**National Institute of
Standards and Technology**
Technology Administration
U.S. Department of Commerce

NIST Special Publication 500-2...

I0004752

Proceedings of Defining the State of the Art in Software Security Tools Workshop

Paul E. Black (workshop chair)
Elizabeth Fong (editor)

Information Technology Laboratory
National Institute of Standards & Technology
Gaithersburg MD 20899

September 2005

U.S. Department of Commerce
Carlos M. Gutierrez. Secretary

Technology Administration
Phillip Bond, Under Secretary of Commerce for Technology

National Institute of Standards and Technology
William Jeffrey, Director

Disclaimer: Any commercial product mentioned is for information only; it does not imply recommendation or endorsement by NIST nor does it imply that the products mentioned are necessarily the best available for the purpose.

Proceedings of
Defining the State of the Art in Software Security Tools Workshop

Paul E. Black (workshop chair)
Elizabeth Fong (editor)
Information Technology Laboratory
National Institute of Standards and Technology
Gaithersburg, MD 20899

ABSTRACT

This proceeding is the result of a workshop held on August 10 and 11, 2005 hosted by the Software Diagnostics and Conformance Testing Division, Information Technology Laboratory, at the National Institute of Standards and Technology. The workshop, "Defining the State of the Art in Software Security Tools," is one of a series in the NIST Software Assurance Measurement and Tool Evaluation (SAMATE) project, which is partially funded by DHS to help identify and enhance software security assurance (SSA) tools. The goal of this workshop is to understand the state of the art of SSA tools that detect security flaws and vulnerabilities and develop a standard reference dataset of programs with known flaws. Forty-five people from outside NIST attended, including representatives from the federal government (NSF, FDA, NSA, DoD, and DHS), seven universities, more than a dozen tool vendors and service providers, and many research companies.

Keywords: Software assessment tools; software assurance; software metrics; software security; reference dataset; vulnerability

Foreword

The workshop on "Defining the State of the Art in Software Security Tools" was held 10-11 August 2005 at the National Institute of Standards and Technology in Gaithersburg, Maryland. Forty-five people from outside NIST attended, including people from government, universities, tool vendors and service providers, and research companies.

For this workshop, members of the workshop committee introduced each session with a brief orientation, then led a discussion among the attendees. The discussions ranged from whether tools and services are commercially viable to if there was enough academic interest and research to how best to encourage more secure software (in both sense) to be developed.

The goals of this workshop were to
- move toward a shared taxonomy of software security flaws and vulnerabilities,
- outline a shared taxonomy of software security assurance (SSA) functions,
- understand the state of the art of SSA tools embodying those functions,
- discuss possible metrics to evaluate the effectiveness of SSA tools, and
- find, collect, and develop a set of flawed and "clean" software to be a standard reference dataset.

Several groups that have been developing taxonomies of security flaws and vulnerabilities exchanged notes and agreed to work together to develop standard nomenclature. Many volunteered to help work toward a standard reference dataset.

These proceedings have five main parts:
- introduction, agenda, etc.,
- position statements and background information from participants,
- discussion material developed by NIST employees,
- extensive notes of the discussions, including the orientations, and
- other material submitted by participants.

Position statements precede the associated participant's background material (the Think-Tank approach) so you can consider the position statement first, discover the source, then reconsider the statement, if warranted.

We thank those who worked to organize this workshop, particularly Elizabeth Fong, who handled much of the correspondence. We are grateful to NIST, especially the Software Diagnostics and Conformance Testing division, for providing the facilities and organizers' time. Special thanks go to Dr. William Spees, FDA, for a very thorough review of the minutes. On behalf of the program committee and the whole SAMATE team, thanks to everyone for taking their time and resources to join us.

Dr. Paul E. Black

Table of Contents

Michael Zhivich, Tim Leek, & Richard Lippmann, "Dynamic Buffer Overflow Detection."

Kendra Kratkiewicz & Richard Lippmann, "Using a Diagnostic Corpus of C Programs to Evaluate Buffer Overflow Detection by Static Analysis Tools."

Thomas W. Reps, Tim Teitelbaum, Paul Anderson, & David Melski, "Static Analysis of Binary Executable Code."

Summary

This is the proceeding of the workshop on Defining the State of the Art in Software Security Tools held on August 10 and 11, 2005. It was hosted by the Software Diagnostics and Conformance Testing Division, Information Technology Laboratory, at the National Institute of Standards and Technology (NIST) in Gaithersburg, MD, USA.

The workshop is one of a series in the NIST Software Assurance Measurement and Tool Evaluation (SAMATE) project, home page http://samate.nist.gov/ Before the workshop the SAMATE team posted discussion material. The workshop consisted of eight sessions:
- Tools survey and categorization
- Taxonomy of software assurance functions
- Recommended best practices, or, state of the art in software assurance tools
- Software assurance (SA) vulnerability list and taxonomy
- Software assurance (SA) tool metrics
- Reference dataset
- Next steps
- Develop consensus of workshop report

Each session had a facilitator who presented orientation material. The pre-workshop discussion material, orientation material for each session, and workshop minutes are included in these proceedings. Here are summaries of the discussions:

- The scope of the tools surveyed was too narrowly focused on just security coding tools and needs to expand to assurance tools which are used in the requirements and design phase of software development life cycle.
- In the session on software assurance functions, discussions centered around the fact the tools do not do the same thing and it is difficult to compare tools. However, most agreed that a specification of tool functions (e.g., detecting buffer overflow) is useful.
- The state of the art of software assurance tools was considered not mature due to lack of knowledge in education and lack of research in how to produce secure software.
- A taxonomy of vulnerabilities is important, however, it will be difficult to achieve "a taxonomy" with properties that everyone will agree on.
- Software metrics and tool metrics are difficult areas and more research is required to develop a set of attributes for measurements.
- There were general consensus that establishing a set of test cases, or reference dataset, was a good idea. Many volunteered to help establish it.
- The workshop concluded with identifying working groups in several areas to begin the process of defining the requirements of SA tool functions and a vulnerability taxonomy, and populating the SAMATE reference dataset.

Workshop Announcement

Defining the State of the Art in Software Security Tools

10 - 11 August 2005, Gaithersburg, Maryland, USA

http://samate.nist.gov/softSecToolsSOA

Organized by the U.S.
National Institute of Standards and Technology (NIST)

Software assurance (SA) tools can help software developers produce software with fewer known security flaws or vulnerabilities. They can also help identify malicious code and poor coding practices that lead to vulnerabilities. There are more than a dozen source code scanners alone, in addition to dozens of other software security tools and services. Reference datasets of clean code and code with security flaws, along with metrics, can help advance the state of the art in software security tools. These metrics and reference datasets can also help purchasers confirm tool vendors' claims. To help develop metrics and reference datasets, the Information Technology Laboratory of the U.S. National Institute of Standards and Technology (NIST) is planning a workshop. One goal of the workshop is to understand the state of the art of SA tools that detect security flaws and vulnerabilities. Participants will also discuss

- possible metrics to evaluate the effectiveness of SA security tools and
- finding, collecting, or developing a set of flawed and "clean" software to be reference code for such evaluation.

As a result of the workshop, we will publish a report on classes of known software security vulnerabilities and the state of the art of security SA tools.

By mid-July, we will publish references to, rough drafts, preliminary versions, or sketches of the following to help generate discussion and comment:

- classes of software security flaws and vulnerabilities,
- a survey of SA security tools and companies,
- the state of the art in SA security tools,
- possible metrics to evaluate SA security tools, and
- a reference set of flawed and "clean" software.

ATTENDANCE and REGISTRATION:

To help us plan the workshop, please send a brief position statement and professional background information. The position statement should address one or more issues in the workshop purpose. The background information should describe your experience this area and your interest, for instance whether you are a vendor, a user, or a researcher of SA security tools. So that we can get you a NIST visitor pass, please include your full name and country of citizenship. If you are not a U.S. citizen, also include your title (e.g., CEO, Program Mgr.), employer/sponsor, and address.

We invite those who develop, use, purchase, or review software security evaluation tools. Academicians who are working in the area of semi- or completely automated tools to review or assess the security properties of software are especially welcome. We are looking for participation from researchers, students, developers, and users in industry, government, and universities.

Send plain text or PDF submissions to Liz Fong <efong@nist.gov>. Your submission constitutes permission for us to publish your position statement and identifying information in workshop proceedings.

SCHEDULE:
    18 June 2005 - Deadline for submission of position statements.
    11 July 2005 - Agenda and references, drafts, sketches, etc. published.
    10-11 August 2005 - Workshop.
    23 September 2005 - Report and proceedings published.

Workshop Chair: Paul E. Black
Program Committee: John Barkely, Elizabeth Fong, Michael Kass, Michael Koo, Brad Martin, and Carl Landwehr

Workshop Agenda

August 10, 2005

9:00 am	Welcoming Remarks	Shashi Phoha, Director, NIST ITL
9:10 am	Round Robin Introductions and Workshop Goals	Paul Black
9:30 am	Tools Survey and Categorization	Facilitator: Elizabeth Fong
10:15 am	Break	
10:25 am	Taxonomy of Software Assurance Functions	Facilitator: Mike Kass
11:30 am	Lunch	
1:00 pm	Recommended Best Practices, or, State of the Art in SA Tools	Facilitator: Brad Martin
2:00 pm	Software Assurance Vulnerability List and Taxonomy	Facilitator: Mike Koo
3:30 pm	Break	
3:45 pm	Software Assurance Tool Metrics	Facilitator: Paul Black
5:00 pm	End of Day 1	

August 11, 2005

9:00 am	Recap of Previous Day	Paul Black
9:15 am	Reference Dataset	Facilitator: Mike Sindelar
10:45 am	Break	
11:00 am	Next Step	Facilitator: Paul Black
11:30 am	Develop Consensus on Workshop Report	Facilitator: Paul Black
12:30pm	End of Workshop	

Attendees

Paul Anderson
GrammaTech, Inc.
paul@grammatech.com

John Barkley
NIST
John.barkley@nist.gov

Sean Barnum
Cigital, Inc
sbarnum@cigital.com

Ryan Berg
Ounce Labs
Ryan.Berg@ouncelabs.com

Joseph I Bergmann
The Open Group
j.bergmann@opengroup.org

Paul E. Black
NIST
Paul.black@nist.gov

Djenana Campara
Klocwork
djenana@klocwork.com

Dave Clauson
Reflective Corporation
dclauson@reflectivecorp.com

Pravir Chandra
Secure Software
Pravir.chandra@securesoftware.org

Brian Chess
Fortify Software
brian@fortifysoftware.com

Steve M. Christey
Mitre Corporation
coley@mitre.org

Patricia Costa
Fraunhofer Center for Experimental
Software Engineering,
pcosta@fc-md.umd.edu

Eric Dalci
NIST
Eric.dalci@nist.gov

Mark Fallon
Oracle Corporation
mark.L.fallon@oracle.com

Brett Fleisch
National Science Foundation
bfleisch@nsf.gov

Elizabeth Fong
NIST
efong@nist.gov

Karen Mercedes Goertzel
Booz Allen Hamilton
goertzel_karen@bah.com

Doug Gooden
CTC Corporation
goodin@ctc.com

Michael W. Hicks
University of Maryland, College Park
mwh@cs.umd.edu

David Jackson
QinetiQ
dmjackson@QinetiQ.com

Joe Jarzombek
Department of Homeland Security
Joe.jarzombek@dhs.gov

Tobie Jones
Booz Allen Hamilton
jones_tobie@bah.com

Michael Kass
NIST
Michael.kass@nist.gov

Michael Koo
NIST
Michael.koo@nist.gov

Richard Lippmann
MIT, Lincoln Laboratory
lippmann@ll.mit.edu

Benjamin Livshits
Stanford Univeresity
livshits@cs.stanford.edu

Brad Martin
NSA
wbmarti@tarius.tycho.ncsc.mil

Robert A. Martin
Mitre Corporation
ramartin@mitre.org

Gary McGraw
Cigital
gem@cigital.com

David Melski
GrammTech, Inc.
melski@grammatech.com

Prateek Mishra
Oracle
Prateek.mishra@oracle.com

Hank Morris
CTC Corporation
morrish@ctc.com

James W. Nash
Nash Laboratories, Inc.
jwn@nashlabs.com

Don O'Neill
Center for National Software Studies
OneillDon@aol.com

Joseph Pamula
George Mason University
Center for Secure Information System
jpamula@gmu.edu

John Peyton
Ounce Labs
John.Peyton@ouncelabs.com

Cody Pierce
Citadel Security Software, Inc.
cpierce@citadel.com

William Worthington Pugh Jr.
University of Maryland, College Park
pugh@cs.umd.edu

Samuel Redwine
James Madison University
redwinst@CISAT.JMU.EDU

Michael Sindelar
NIST
michael.sindelar@nist.gov

William S. Spees
USA CDRH (FDA)
wss@cdrh.fda.gov

Pedro Vales
Concurrent Technologies
valesp@ctc.com

Larry D. Wagoner
DOD
l.wagone@radium.ncsc.mil

Andrew White
National Security Agency
awhite@empire.eclipse.ncsc.mil

Dave Wichers
Aspect Security
Dave.wichers@aspectsecurity.com

Theodore Winograd
Booz Allen Hamilton
winograd_theodore@bah.com

Stan Wisseman, CISP, CISM
Booz Allen Hamilton
wisseman_stan@bah.com

Chris Wysopal
Symantec Corporation
cwysopal@gmail.com

Kenneth R. van Wyk
Krvw Associates
ken@krvw.com

Marvin Zelkowitz
University of Maryland and
Fraunhofer Center for Experimental
Software Engineering, MD
marv@zelkowitz.com

Position Statements and Background Information

This section contains the position statements and background information that have been submitted by the workshop participants. Some participants did not submit position statements or biographical information and, therefore, these are omitted. Some submitted materials but did not attend the workshop; their materials are included in this document. Some also submitted papers; and these are included in the section "Submitted Material".

Position Statement 1

Present software security state-of-the-art can be divided into existing commercial tools, existing research efforts (near-term-future tools), and practices & procedures. Of these three, the first currently focuses largely on signature-based "unsafe function" detection (e.g. the much-reviled sprintf() with its lack of boundary checking), with a secondary emphasis on tracking the flow of "tainted" data. These are effective at identifying a subset of vulnerabilities, particularly those of certain buffer overflows and SQL injection attacks, but are subject to significant false-positive reporting and miss nearly identical vulnerabilities where a signed function is written by hand, or where taint-checking functions are flawed but trusted by the tools. The second category of efforts, current research, again focus largely on buffer and stack overflows; practices & procedures offer a wider scope of checking with human intelligence in a code review (whether an audit committee, or a lighter review system such as the "extreme programming" buddy system or open-source model "approver" role), as well as managerial visibility in tracking and trending statistics. The practices & procedures are slowly moving from state-of-art to state-of-practice, led largely by open-source and small-practice consulting teams; tools are being adopted but yet more slowly, and typically by larger, more affluent organizations.

These are positive measures, and can be shown to help reduce large classes of defects of the sort that have been exploited by hackers and worm-writers. However, considering the full spectrum of possible software attack, these are effective only in closing a portion of the "accidental vulnerability" set, and many are effectively only with access to source code. Thus, end customers remain largely ignorant of the vulnerability status of products they buy, and integrators may be ignorant of vulnerabilities in binary components (e.g. software libraries) they use in their products. Moreover, "deliberate vulnerabilities"--- whether back doors designed benignly for debugging and maintenance, or more maliciously constructed functions---cannot be detected, because today's tools cannot differentiate those mis-features from legitimate functionality.

This suggests the need for an emphasis on binary code analysis and/or decompilation for analysis, accessible even to informed end-users without source code, and on the need for tools that cross-check implementation against the designed intent of software.

Recognizing that both are very hard problems, there will otherwise be large classes of vulnerabilities that cannot be detected, and less external incentive for vendors to ensure that their products pass testing.

Mr. Freeland Abbott
Georgia Tech Research Institute
Freeland.Abbott@gtri.gatech.edu

Mr. Freeland Abbott is a research scientist at the Georgia Tech Research Institute, with a degree in computer science & engineering from MIT. He has been a professional developer of several complex software systems for about 15 years. At GTRI, under contract to the Joint Systems Integration Command, he recently conducted an analysis source code assessment tools, and smaller "quick look" assessments of related products, which has re-energized his earlier interest in compilers, debuggers, and verification tools. As a software engineer, Mr. Abbott has interest and background in techniques and processes for software design and quality assurance generally, as well as security and vulnerability minimization specifically.

Position Statement 2

The Context. A substantial percentage of all US coding jobs will be outsourced to China, Israel, Russia, the E.U., and India in the coming decade. On top of the trend toward outsourcing, there is increasing deployment of COTS software—for which source code is often unavailable—in presumably secure national and DoD information systems. Moreover, legacy code—for which design documents are usually out-of-date, and for which source code is sometimes unavailable and sometimes non-existent—will continue to be left deployed.

The Problem. What is needed are ways to determine whether third-party and legacy application programs can perform malicious operations (or can be induced to perform malicious operations), and to be able to make such judgments in the absence of source code.

(A full paper by Thomas W. Reps, Tim Teitelbaum, Paul Anderson, and David Melski, entitled "Static Analysis of Binary Executable Code," is included in this document under the section called Submitted Material.)

Dr. Paul Anderson and Dr. David Melski
GrammaTech, Inc.
paul@grammatech.com
melski@grammatech.com

Dr. Anderson is a Senior Software Scientist at GrammaTech. He received his B.Sc. from Kings College, University of London in 1985 and his Ph.D. from City University London in 1991. Anderson has been a Senior Software Engineer at GrammaTech since July 1991, where he has been responsible for both the design of GrammaTech's commercial products and conducting government sponsored research. Part of his responsibilities includes lead product developer for CodeSurfer (a code-understanding tool based on program analysis) and CodeSonar (a program analysis tool for finding software flaws). Anderson was the principle investigator for the Phase-II SBIR "Detecting Malicious Code in Firmware," that leads to the development of CodeSurfer/x86, the premier machine-code analysis tool. He is currently principle investigator of an SBIR project on, "Sanitizing Software of Malicious and Unauthorized Code." Dr. Anderson's research has been reported in numerous articles, journal publications, book chapters, and international conferences.

Dr. Melski is a Senior Software Scientist at GrammaTech. Melski graduated summa cum laude from the University of Wisconsin in 1994 with a B.S. in Computer Sciences and Russian Studies. He received his Ph.D. in Computer Sciences from the University of Wisconsin in 2002. Melski was the principle investigator on the Phase-II SBIR, "Source Code Vulnerability Detection," that lead to the development of CodeSonar and the Path Inspector (a software model checker). He has been involved in the development of CodeSurfer/x86, and is the principle investigator on several projects related to CodeSurfer/x86, including: "Modernization of Legacy Software" (decompilation), "Defenses Against Reverse Engineering," and "Defenses Against Malicious Code". He is the principle investigator on a NASA-funded project on "Practical Model Checking to Enforce Domain-Specific Interfaces and Requirements," and a technical lead on an HSARPA-funded project on, "Model Checking Software Binaries."

Position Statement 3

The next great wave in software development is sure to be in the area of software security. As reliability, scalability, maintainability and the other -ilities have now become de rigueur considerations for development professionals, security in the software world has long been considered a network or deployed application level issue rather than a core systemic one. Today, the ever-growing complexity of software systems combined with the rising business impact of failure of these systems from a security perspective, is pushing software security considerations from the perimeter into the center of software development considerations. It is no longer adequate to worry about security issues after the fact. Rather, building security into the software as part of the underlying SDLC from beginning to end is quickly becoming a fundamental assumption. Part of this awakening of security as part of the SDLC has been the growing emergence of new and powerful tools to support security assurance as a first-tier consideration in software development.

As Software Assurance tools become more and more capable and prevalent, it is important to note that all of these tools are only as valuable as the pool of knowledge that they are applying, validating and automating. A primary example of this is the case of static code analysis tools and the sets of security rules that they check for. The two key differentiators between tools in this space are the nature of scanning they are capable of (simple lexical scanning, constructive parsing, data flow analysis, etc.) and the breadth and depth of rules that they scan for. If you performed a comprehensive analysis of the rule sets for all the tools available today, you would quickly discover a substantial level of overlap from tool to tool. It is a key concern of mine to work toward a consensus understanding of what these security rules are and how they fit into the broader security knowledge architecture, and to gain standardization of an internal schematic structure for rules and an independent, portable method of representing rules for tool consumption. Through such efforts at consensus and standardization, we move the field of software security forward in a unified manner, ensure more appropriate levels of tool interoperability and reduce the burden for software development professionals to truly adopt and embrace the practices of software security.

Sean Barnum
Director of Knowledge Management
Cigital, Inc
sbarnum@cigital.com

Sean Barnum is a management professional with over eighteen years of experience in the software and broader technology industries. In that time, his experience has covered a wide range of technical domains from consumer oriented software development to telecommunications embedded systems to business and IT consulting. Throughout these experiences his consistent passion has been in the practice of continuous improvement. This passion has fueled his involvement in Software QA, Enterprise Quality Management, Process Management & Improvement and most recently into Knowledge Management which he believes forms the tie that binds all the rest together. Barnum is currently Director of Knowledge Management for Cigital, a leading software consulting firm specializing in designing and implementing software security and quality delivery improvement programs and enterprise application management solutions. This role gives him direct responsibility for company process improvement, collaboration and enterprise information management including the definition and implementation of knowledge architectures and catalogs to support the company's primary domains of expertise: Software Security, Software Quality and Software Development Process Improvement. His current interests and activities include software security knowledge & practices, risk management, software quality and process improvement, and collaborative technologies among others. Barnum has a BS in computer science from Portland State University. He is a member of the IEEE Computer Society and OASIS, and is involved in numerous knowledge standards-defining efforts.

Position Statement 4

In our work at Ounce Labs, and we believe in the work ahead in this workshop, it is vitally important to consider the issue of software vulnerabilities from a risk management perspective. While zero vulnerabilities would be of course ideal, the preponderance of legacy code and the pressures of budgets, development schedules, and deliverables mean we must provide specific, measurable, repeatable ways for the user community and management to make informed, reasonable risk management decisions about their software vulnerability, both inside the development lifecycle and in production. This implies that deriving a usable vulnerability metric is vitally important to provide a standard benchmark for evaluation and trends analysis. It also implies that tools and processes must consider vulnerabilities in their fullest sense; that is, not only the vulnerabilities introduced through coding errors, but also design flaws and violations of policy that result in insufficient protections and monitoring in code, such as encryption, access control, and the like.

We must, while striving for the ideal, provide concrete, measurable, consistent steps to help professionals understand the risk within their organization, prioritize response, and measure progress. Ultimately, arriving at a common vocabulary for identifying, describing, and addressing this total range of vulnerabilities will help the wider community most effectively and efficiently address their overall software risk.

Ryan Berg, Co-Founder and Lead Security Architect
Ounce Labs, Inc.
Ryan.berg@ouncelabs.com

John Peyton, Co-Founder and Principal Architect
Ounce Labs, Inc
john.peyton@ouncelabs.com

Ryan Berg is a Co-Founder and Lead Security Architect of Ounce Labs, Inc., innovator of software vulnerability risk management solutions, based in Waltham, MA. Prior to Ounce, Ryan co-founded Qiave Technologies, a pioneer in kernel-level security, which later sold to WatchGuard Technologies in October of 2000. Ryan also served as a Senior Software Engineer at GTE Internetworking, leading the architecture and implementation of new managed firewall services. Ryan holds patents and patents pending in, multi-language security assessment, intermediary security assessment language, communication protocols, and security management systems.

John Peyton is a Software Engineer and Architect of Ounce Labs, Inc., innovator of software security assurance solutions, based in Waltham, MA. Prior to Ounce, John was a Design Architect for language independent intermediate representation, targeting highly optimizing compilers for Hewlett-Packard. John also served as a representative to the ANSI C committee for Apollo Computer and Hewlett-Packard. With more than 18 years industry experience in compiler development, John is a joint patent-holder for advanced optimization techniques across large program regions, as well as co-author of "A C User's Guide to ANSI C".

Position Statement 5

Within the RTES Forum we have two activities that might be of interest to you and your colleagues --1) Security for RTES and 2) High Assurance in Safety Critical

Environments. Under number 1 we have a Generic Protection Profile at the NSA for review at EAL 6 Plus. This is a collaborative work with the OMG and others.

Joseph Bergmann
The Open Group
j.Bergmann@opengroup.org

I am the Director of Real-time and Embedded Systems Forum of The Open Group.

Position Statement 6

The best benchmarks serve non-experts by producing simple, easy-to-compare results regardless of the complexity of the solution. I propose the following three principles for creating a benchmark for bug detection:

1) Take the user's perspective. A bug detection benchmark should measure the following properties of a tool above all else:

- Ability to detect an explicit set of bugs that the community deems important.
- Ability to produce output that can be consumed efficiently (often expressed as "give me few false alarms").
- Performance (both capacity and execution time).

2) Name the scenario. Consider the TPC-C benchmark, the most widely used standard for evaluating database performance: In the TPC-C business model, a wholesale parts supplier (called the Company below) operates out of a number of warehouses and their associated sales districts. Each warehouse in the TPC- C model must supply ten sales districts, and each district serves three thousand customers. An operator from a sales district can select, at any time, one of the five operations or transactions offered by the Company's order-entry system. (From http://www.tpc.org/tpcc/detail.asp)

For bug detection tools, interesting scenarios might include:
- A network server that speaks a standard protocol (http, ftp, smtp, etc.)
- A set of device drivers
- A web-based enterprise application
- A privileged system utility.

3) Start with documented bugs (and their solutions). The body of open source applications is large enough and rich enough that a bug detection benchmark should never suffer the complaint that the included bugs do not represent realistic practices or coding styles. The benchmark code need not be drawn verbatim from open source applications, but the pedigree of a each bug should be documented as part of the benchmark. Because false alarms are such a concern, the benchmark should include code that represents both a bug and the fix for the bug.

Creating a benchmark is hard. It requires making value judgments about what is important, what is less important, and what can be altogether elided. These judgments are harder still for people who value precision, since computing a benchmark result will invariably require throwing some precision away. We should not expect to get it all right the first time. Any successful benchmark will inevitably evolve in scope, content, and methodology. The best thing we can do is making a start.

Dr. Brian Chess
Chief Scientist, Fortify Software
brian@fortifysoftware.com

Brian's research focuses on methods for identifying security vulnerabilities in software. He received his Ph.D. from the University of California at Santa Cruz, where he began applying his work in integrated circuit test and verification to the problem of software security. His efforts culminated in the development of Eau Claire, a framework for detecting and eliminating security vulnerabilities in software. In addition to being a published researcher, Brian has delivered in the commercial software arena, having led development efforts at Hewlett Packard and NetLedger.

Position Statement 7

Regardless of the technology used to improve software security, the biggest barrier to successful developer adoption of these tools is communication. The communication gap between those who are creating security policies for their product development teams or IT organizations and those who must ultimately implement that policy - the software developers - is difficult to overcome. In order to close this gap, organizations must communicate to developers in a language they understand and in an environment that they use everyday. Klocwork believes the use of a 'security compiler' that sits on the developer desktop, and which communicates and enforces security policy is the best method to leverage automated analysis to meet the organization's security goals.

Djenana Campara
CTO, Chairwoman of the Board, Klocwork
"Djenana Campara" <djenana@klocwork.com>

Djenana founded Klocwork in 2001 after successfully spinning it out of Nortel Networks and establishing it as an independent company. As a pioneer in static software code analysis, Djenana brings 19 years of software experience to the role of CTO at Klocwork, and has been awarded four US patents for her groundbreaking software development work in creating Klocwork inSight. Ms.Campara co-chairs the Object Management Group (OMG) Architecture-Driven Modernization Task Force, and serves as a board member on the Canadian Consortium of Software Engineering Research (CSER). She has published several papers on software transformations, has been quoted in publications, including The Economist, and has participated in Fortune Magazine's "Brainstorm 2003," an international conference of the world's most creative leaders.

Position Statement 8

Reflective is a software security and code quality assurance provider. As a company, we are focusing a great deal of energy on software quality metrics particularly as they relate to security issues. As such, the focus of this workshop would be very interesting for us and relevant to our customer needs. While we did not submit a position paper, our experience with customers such as ISS, Narus and Siebel has given us a wealth of customer insight into the issues surrounding software security and the use of metrics in establishing baselines for code quality and security. We would look forward to being an active participant in the discussions.

Dave Clauson Reflective Corporation Carriage House 1444 Fairview Road Atlanta, GA 30306-4012 dclauson@reflectivecorp.com

With a background that includes over twenty-five years of experience in development and deployment of technology-driven products and services, Dave Clauson combines the discipline of market-driven thinking together with a passion for breakthrough ideas. Seeing the move towards outsourced application development and the need for new technology for checking source code, Dave founded Reflective, the first company to provide an automated source code security test and management system. As Founder and CEO of Reflective, Dave's mission is to rewrite the rules for how companies protect, test and manage one of their most critical business assets – their source code.

Prior to joining Reflective, Dave was a co-founder of two security technology companies. CloudShield developed the first optical network packet processor - a breakthrough product with significant applications in high speed network security. Dave was also the first Chief Marketing Officer for ArcSight, a leading risk management software provider for companies seeking to prioritize security event correlation. Both start-ups were developed by SVIC, a Silicon Valley venture capital firm that Dave helped start.

Clauson, an honors graduate of UCLA, has advised the 4A's, the CTIA and the NAB on technology issues and legislation that might impact the marketing of technology goods and services. He has testified as an expert witness before the Federal Trade Commission on privacy and the Internet and served as an advisor to the President's Council on the Internet.

Regardless of where technology goes, expect Dave to be working hard to develop new ideas and companies that will help generate value from it.

Position Statement 9

Oracle is an advocate for software industry use of security assurance tools as part of a defense-in-depth strategy to develop products more securely. A government procurement requirement for use of these tools would greatly improve the assurance of commercial software, provided that these tools are mature enough and usable (e.g. with very low false positive rates and high scalability). We recommend a formal certification process to validate effectiveness and usability.

Mark Fallon
Oracle Corporation
mark.fallon@oracle.com

Mark Fallon is a senior release manager at Oracle and is primarily responsible for Oracle Database. In this role, he helps drive secure development initiatives within Oracle's Server Technologies division. Mr. Fallon has been with Oracle for six years, starting with porting of Oracle Real Application Clusters, then managing the JavaVM, pre-compiler porting group, and later release managing all the Unix-based database ports, finally moving to the release management group in base development.

Prior to joining Oracle, Mr. Fallon, was a researcher at Hitachi's Dublin Laboratory, working in the parallel computing area. He represented Hitachi to the MPI Standard Forum, and later worked with National Institute of Science and Technology on interoperableMPI

Mr. Fallon has a Bachelor of Arts, Moderatorship and Master of Science in Computer Science from Trinity College, Dublin.

Position Statement 10

Need to establish software assurance for tools development: Software assurance issues are just as relevant for the tools being used to test software security as they are for the software being tested. The ability to trust the output of a security testing tools is directly proportional to the ability to establish the assurance of the integrity of that tool, in terms of its non-subversion either by its supplier before delivery or by a malicious tester or third-party attacker after deployment.

- Need multiple tools/techniques for adequate coverage: No single tool can provide enough coverage to be effective in assessing the security flaws or vulnerabilities of a whole software system, an individual component, or even a single module. A combination of both "white box" (source code analysis) and "black box" (binary executable testing/assessment) techniques, and tools to support those techniques, is needed to achieve adequate coverage.

- Code analysis has noteworthy limitations: Code analysis only covers a very small piece of the overall software security testing objective. It is constrained because:

  a. It presumes the source code is available to be analyzed.

  b. The analysis technique is static, and limited to identifying known syntactical flaws and, to a limited extent, implementation flaws in interfaces/interactions within a single source code module.

  c. It does not enable the tester to observe the software's behavior, particularly in terms of its interactions with other entities, handling of environment inputs, etc.

  d. Its quality is highly dependent on the expertise, meticulousness, and stamina of the analyst. Automated tools help only to the extent that they can help point the analyst to "suspicious" parts of code, and thus possibly help reduce level of effort.

- "Black box" test tools are more versatile than "white box" test tools: The security testing/assessment tools for binary software are also useful for compiled source code. The reverse is not true: source code analysis tools are useless when the software to be assessed is a binary executable, e.g., a COTS component. For this reason, more future research should focus on improving the range and quality of black box tools.

- Penetration testing should be augmented by other black box techniques: Penetration testing, the most "established" binary assessment technique, with or without tools, is only as good as the expertise, imagination, and stamina of the testers, and the tools, resources, and time available to the them. Pen testing should be augmented (not replaced) by other "black box" security testing techniques, such as security fault injection and automated vulnerability scanning.

- Emerging tools only scratch the surface of what is still needed for comprehensive software security testing: There are a number of interesting emerging tools designed to fill in the gaps in test coverage, these only add a few more pieces to the jigsaw puzzle. If tools are to be relied on to automate most security testing, much more is needed.

- Need standard evaluation criteria and techniques for tools selection: Comprehensive standard set of evaluation criteria - technical and non-technical - so that tools suppliers could know in advance minimum requirements for their tools. In addition, a standard set of tools rating metrics for use by evaluators, and a set of "best practices" outlining robust techniques for evaluation of testing tools.

- Need tools to automate test planning: Tools are needed to help automate creation of test/misuse cases, test scenarios, test oracles, etc.

- Need methodology for determining best combination of tools/techniques: Methodology would first determine the best combination of techniques to achieve necessary coverage, based on an analysis of the known characteristics of the software to be tested and the test environment. Methodology would then map appropriate combination of tools to those techniques. Methodology would then refine list of tools/techniques based on known time, resource, tester expertise, and other key constraints.

- Need a range of tools and middleware to enable correlation and fusion of test results: This is needed to support analysis of test results cross whole software systems, and for larger objectives of integrated "security situational awareness" and risk management.

- Need a graphical tool to depict fused test results: A tool that can capture the results from multiple test tools, correlate and plot those results on a graphical software architecture "map" so testers can easily see the points throughout the software system where flaws/vulnerabilities have been detected.

- Need a translation tool to support easy tester comprehension of results across tools: Translator would produce a fused test report including a table expressing each test tool result in multiple standard and common proprietary flaw/vulnerability description languages (e.g., AVDL, OVAL, proprietary), thus alleviating the tester's need to learn multiple description language syntaxes, and also providing a basis for correlating outputs from different test tools/techniques as the basis for defining a standard for test tool output format and syntax.

- Need a "super repository" of known flaws/vulnerabilities: Need to establish (through data mining?) an extensive, comprehensive Super Repository of software security flaws/vulnerabilities that collects and correlates the flaws/vulnerabilities stored across multiple recognized vulnerability and flaw databases, such as CVE, Bugtraq, etc.

- Need to determine how tools from other software disciplines can be applied: Research how tools from the QA, safety, and fault-tolerance communities can be applied to security testing, in order to expand the coverage and nature of tests.

- Need methodology for dealing with false positive/false negatives in tools results: Development of algorithm-based methodology to analyze test results collected over time from a single tool, in order to trends in the rates of false positives and false negatives for each finding type. This will enable (1) the tool supplier to improve the accuracy of the tool; (2) testers who analyze results from the tool to refined those results as necessary to compensate for predictable inaccuracies.

- Need middleware to automate series of tests using multiple tools: Tools middleware to establish linkages among security test tools in order to automate an entire test scenario that combines use of multiple tools.

23

- Need interfaces to risk analysis, intrusion detection, configuration management, etc.: Middleware providing interfaces to refine (reformat, etc.) and "feed" tools output into risk analysis tool repositories, configuration management repositories, intrusion detection/sensor databases, etc., in support of a wider vision of "integrated security situational awareness".

- Need "historical database" of test results for trends analysis: Capability for archiving test results into a repository in a format that will be meaningful to later analysts (i.e., not requiring direct involvement with the tests for comprehension). Along with this repository is needed a tool that can analyze the results collected over time, and produce metrics of observed trends, for example differences in test results of a module before and after flaw remediation, differences between component versions, etc. Such metrics can be used to directly inform the risk management process.

- Need tools to support patch and update risk management: Tools to support automated post-update impact analysis and patch security regression testing.

Karen Goertzel, CISSP
Booz Allen Hamilton - H5061
goertzel_karen@bah.com

Theodore Winograd
Booz Allen Hamilton
WINOGRAD_THEODORE@bah.com

Tobie Jones
Booz Allen Hamilton
<jones_tobie@bah.com>

Ms. Goertzel has over 23 years of experience in analysis, research, systems engineering, and technical writing. Her main area of technical expertise is information assurance, with specializations in software assurance and cross-domain solutions. In addition to a wide range of other activities in this area, Ms. Goertzel acts as the software security subject matter expert in support of the Director of the Department of Homeland Security Software Assurance Initiative. From 2002-2004, Ms. Goertzel was the technical program manager and lead contributor for the Defense Information Systems Agency's Application Security Project, in which she led a team analysts and software developers in the creation and ongoing enhancement of guidance documents defining process improvements, methodologies, and techniques for ensuring that software security was considered when defining, procuring, developing, and deploying software components and systems. The DISA project also defined a software security testing/vulnerability assessment tools taxonomy, and selection criteria for evaluating candidate tools. These criteria were then used to evaluate and select a set of security code scanners, application vulnerability scanners, and security fault injection tools, to be combined into a toolkit; a methodology for use of the toolkit in performing software security assessments was also developed. Before joining Booz Allen Hamilton, Ms. Goertzel was a technical consultant/requirements analyst in the area of cross-domain solutions and high-assurance trusted systems for Honeywell Federal Systems/HFSI/Wang Federal/Getronics Government Solutions (now BAE/DigitalNet). Before joining Honeywell, Ms. Goertzel was a technical writer for Cellular Radio Corporation, Omnicom, GuideStar, Perceptronics, C.I.T. Alcatel, Input/Ouput Computer Systems (IOCS), and Young & Associates.

Mr. Winograd's main area of expertise is in information assurance with a specialization in software assurance. In 2004, under the Defense Information Systems Agency's Application Security Project, Mr. Winograd created and enhanced guidance for properly implementing software security techniques, methodologies, and mechanisms in the development of software applications. Additionally, Mr. Winograd led the effort to select and evaluate a variety of software assurance tools for inclusion in a toolkit. To that end, he aided in the definition of the evaluation criteria and methodology. Additionally, he developed methodologies for using the tools when performing software security assessments. His interests lie in the analysis of tools, development of mechanisms, and provision of guidance.

Ms. Jones has over six years of software development experience in industry as well as invaluable experience and knowledge of software engineering processes and methodologies gained in post-secondary education and on-the-job performance. Her primary functions are in the area of information assurance, specializing in software assurance. In 2004, she was the lead analyst performing a secure code review for the DoD Defense Personnel Records Imaging System (DPRIS) Web interface. Additionally, under the Defense Information Systems Agency's Application Security Project, Ms. Jones provided analysis, research and technical writing in support of development of guidance for secure software implementation, acquisition, testing and deployment. Ms. Jones' other work and professional interests in software security encompass a range of activities including technical writing and research, analysis, design and development.

Position Statement 11

It is my belief that software analysis tools can be of significant benefit in improving the security and reliability of software. Many tools have already been developed that detect security vulnerabilities, such as buffer overruns, "time-of-check-to-time-of-use" violations, and leaks of possibility sensitive information. Other tools detect security-relevant bugs, like deadlocks, race conditions, dangling pointer dereferences, memory leaks and others. All of these problems can be quite difficult to discover though manual analysis or testing, and so using automated tools seems a promising approach.

To make progress in developing tools of use to a wide clientele, we need to develop metrics and benchmarks with which to evaluate software analysis tools. An important tradeoff of all software analysis tools is soundness vs. completeness. A sound tool will report all *possible* violations of a given property, but some warnings will be false alarms. On the other hand, a complete tool will report only *actual* violations, but may fail to report all possible problems. Since software analysis in general cannot be both sound and complete (due to Rice's theorem), tool designers are faced with an important tradeoff: a sound tool that reports too many warnings is of little use, because the process of sifting through the warnings quickly degenerates into a tedious form of code review. But an unsound tool will miss violations, meaning that the program could still contain important vulnerabilities.

The question of soundness vs. completeness is one metric of expressiveness: how well can a tool discover a particular problem?

There are other important metrics as well, such usability, scalability (will it work for large programs?), customizability, and others. I believe an important outcome of the workshop will be to (1) identify security problems for which tools seem like a good approach, and (2) list metrics by which we might evaluate and compare such tools.

Once the metrics have been established, and tradeoffs have been identified between them for particular problems, we need ways to evaluate how well tools satisfy the relevant metrics. A useful way to do this is to establish benchmark suites of software that contain known vulnerabilities, to see how effectively tools discover those vulnerabilities. For example, are all the vulnerabilities reported?

How many false alarms are there? How fast does the tool run (if at all)? How quickly can a trained user find problems, or suppress false alarms, when using the tool? The important challenge in coming up with benchmarks is that security holes are hard to find! That is, while we may know of some security holes in programs, there may be problems yet to be discovered. Another problem is obtaining source code for important programs for those tools that need it. While there is much open source code available now, there may not be an open source version of a particular category of program.

Michael W. Hicks
Assistant Professor
Department of Computer Science and Institute of Advanced Computer Studies
University of Maryland, College Park
Michael Hicks <mwh@cs.umd.edu>

My main research interest is in developing new languages or language analyses to improve the quality of software. I am a principal designer and developer of the programming language Cyclone, which is a variant of the popular language C, but designed to be "safe." Cyclone prevents the possibility of common security holes like buffer overruns, while still providing the high degree of programmer control familiar to C programmers but not available in languages like Java. I have also developed tools to statically detect interface transparency violations in Java programs, and to discover data races in C programs (via static analysis) and Java programs (via dynamic and static analysis in combination). I have recently started to explore means to prove that programs exhibit certain security properties, like confidentiality and integrity. In all my work, I use semantic techniques to theoretically model programming languages and their relevant properties, and then build tools to analyze actual programs to see how well the theory translates to practice.

Position Statement 12

The QinetiQ Systems Assurance Group has at least a 25 year history in the research of technology to support software and systems assurance. This goes back to days when this part of QinetiQ was the Royal Signals and Radar Establishment (RSRE), a research organisation forming part of the UK Ministry of Defence. As part of RSRE this group had an interest in computer security and sound software construction, international collaborations in this area were part of The Technical Co-Operation Programme, TTCP, through a group led by Carl Landwehr. Since then, work has been targeted at Safety Critical Software with the development of tools to analyse a wide range of languages, including Ada, C and 68000. These tools have been used to provide safety certification evidence for military systems such as a missile decoy system and the European Fighter Aircraft. The tools are now being exploited in new domains including security and reliability; for example, the Apache web server has been analysed for security vulnerabilities. Research and early tool development is expanding into the assurance of systems of systems and the composition of tools to provide scalable system wide assurance.

This work is complemented by the security health check service also within QTIM; this service examines clients' systems for any security vulnerabilities and, as part of this service, it maintains a list of known security vulnerabilities. Our long involvement in the security of defence systems has led to the 'Domain Based Security' model, adopted by the UK Ministry of Defence, for expressing and realizing security requirements; this has inspired a collection of system components (SyBard) to help in the realisation of those requirements.

His recent activities (whilst working for Praxis HIS Ltd) include leading a study into the application of tools to Common Criteria software assessment. The study included a survey of tool categories, assessment of potential benefits for developers and evaluators, and proposals for changes to working practices and assurance approaches. (A summary of the results of the study is available at http://www.cesg.gov.uk/site/iacs/itsec/media/techniques_tools/eval4_study.pdf)

David has almost twenty years' experience in high-quality software engineering technical consultancy and project management, with a particular focus on the definition and development of high-integrity systems. He has worked in the aerospace, telecommunications, automotive, rail, nuclear, and healthcare industries; his clients have included major manufacturers, system developers, regulators and government agencies, in the UK, mainland Europe and the USA.

David Jackson
QinetiQ Systems
dmjackson@qinetiq.com

David Jackson is a Senior Consultant with QinetiQ Trusted Information Management (QTIM) Systems Assurance Group. His professional interests include development and application of tools for building and assuring high-integrity security & safety systems, rigorous development methods, and techniques for managing the risk of system engineering programmes.

Position Statement 13

We plan to attend the NIST Software Security Tools workshop and have recently finished evaluations of static analysis tools (Polyspace, SPLINT, ARCHER, UNO, BOON) and dynamic test/instrumentation tools (CCured, CRED, Insure++, ProPolice, TinyCC, Chaperon, Valgrind) that detect buffer overflows. We have two 6-10 page summaries of these evaluations and could submit them as position papers. These papers describe corpora that were developed, how the evaluations were performed, a taxonomy that can be used to describe buffer overflows, and the performance of different tools.

(2 papers were received from Lippmann and are included in this document under the section called Submitted Material.)

Dr. Richard Lippmann
MIT, Lincoln Laboratory
lippmann@ll.mit.edu

I am a Senior Staff member at MIT Lincoln Laboratory performing research on detecting and eliminating vulnerabilites in Internet software. Recent studies at Lincoln Laboratory have created two databases to evaluate the ability of commercial and open source static analysis and dynamic testing tools to find buffer overflows in C Internet server software. One database is available from http://www.ll.mit.edu/IST/corpora.html and a second is available by sending email to Kendra Kratkiewicz (kendra@ll.mit.edu). Results of studies performed using these databases are presented in the two papers submitted to this workshop. It was found that most static analysis tools cannot be applied to large Internet server C source code and that most have high false alarm rates and/or low detection rates. Dynamic testing tools perform better, but require test cases to reveal buffer overflows. We are currently exploring approaches to combine the advantages of dynamic testing and static analysis.

Position Statement 14

A recent explosion in the number of security vulnerabilities being discovered every day motivated a great deal of interest in tools that attempt to address this problem. While buffer overruns have been plaguing C programs for years, application-level vulnerabilities such as SQL injections, cross-site scripting, and path traversal attacks have become increasingly common in the last year. Looking at a daily snapshot of Security-Focus vulnerabilities reveals that upwards of 60% of all exploits are due to application vulnerabilities such as the ones listed above.

While the number of commercially available and open-source tools that claim to address these issues is on the rise, there is generally no approach that would validate the claims made by the tool makers. We believe that there is a need for a set of universally accepted benchmarks that can be used as a validation test bed for security tools. Putting together such a set of realistic benchmarks is challenging because many if not most applications suffering from application-level vulnerabilities are closed-source proprietary software deployed at banks, medical centers, etc. While some attempts have been made at constructing artificial benchmarks [1, 4], we believe that real-life programs are much better suited for testing security tools.

In the course of our research in application security [3] at Stanford, our group has developed a suite of benchmarks called STANFORD SECURIBENCH [2]. Thus far it consists of 8 real-life open-source Web-based applications written in Java and developed on top of J2EE. Most programs are medium-sized, with the larger ones consisting of almost 200,000 lines of code. We have identified about 30 vulnerabilities in these programs and there are probably more that can be found with appropriate static and dynamic tools.

We are making these benchmarks publicly available in hopes of fostering collaboration between researchers. These benchmarks can serve as test cases for researchers and industry practitioners working in this area.

References
[1] Foundstone, Inc. Hacme books, test application for Web security. http://www.foundstone.com/index.htm?subnav=resources/navigation.htm&subcontent=/resources/oddesc/hacmebooks.htm.
[2] Benjamin Livshits. Stanford SecuriBench. http://suif.stanford.edu/_livshits/securibench/, 2005.
[3] V. Benjamin Livshits and Monica S. Lam. Finding security errors in Java programs with static analysis. In *Proceedings of the 2005 Usenix Security Conference*, 2005.
[4] The Open Web Application Security Project. WebGoat Project. http://www.owasp.org/software/webgoat.html.

Benjamin Livshits
Stanford Univeresity
livshits@cs.stanford.edu

Benjamin Livshits is a Ph.D. candidate in computer science at Stanford University. Benjamin graduated summa cum laude with a B.A. degree in computer science and math from Cornell University in 1999. He obtained an M.S. from Stanford University in 2002.

Benjamin's general research area is compilers and program analysis. His research interests include applications of static and dynamic analysis techniques to finding errors in programs. Lately he has focused on techniques for finding buffer overruns in C programs and a variety of security vulnerabilities in Web-based applications written in Java. Benjamin has authored several papers on program analysis for security and other uses, including finding memory errors, violated API-specific patterns, software pattern mining, etc.

Position Statement 15

Through research and collaboration with industry and academia, I and my co-workers are working to establish a formal set of Common Flaw Types for the entire collection of over 12,000 publicly known CVE Names, which continues to grow 70-100 each week. We are interested in working with the community to create definitions and descriptions of these Common Flaw Types, and we will be exploring what type of code exemplars (patterns, code snippets, etc.) would be needed to allow tools to be trained to identify the Common Flaw Types in source code, and finally we will be exploring verification methods to determine appropriate methods and mechanisms for verifying the effectiveness of these types of source code assessment tools.

Robert Alan Martin
Mitre Corporation
"Robert A. Martin" ramartin@mitre.org

Steve M. Christey
Mitre Corporation
coley@mitre.org

Robert Martin is the primary point of contact for the Common Vulnerabilities and Exposures (CVE) Compatibility efforts, a member of the Open Vulnerability and Assessment Language (OVAL) team, and a Principal Engineer in MITRE's Information Technologies Directorate. For the past five years, Robert's efforts have been focused on the interplay of cyber security, critical infrastructure protection, and the use of software-based technologies and services. Prior to these efforts, Robert developed a standardized software quality assessment process that is still being used to help MITRE's Air Force, Army, and FAA customers improve their software acquisition methods as well as the quality, cost, and timeliness of their delivered software products. To-date, over 121 projects have been assessed through Robert's Software Quality Assessment Exercise (SQAE). Robert joined the MITRE Corporation in 1981 after earning a bachelor's degree and a master's degree in electrical engineering from Rensselaer Polytechnic Institute, subsequently he earned a master's of business degree from Babson College. He is a member of the ACM, AFCEA, IEEE, and the IEEE Computer Society.

Steve M. Christey is the editor of the Common Vulnerabilities and Exposures (CVE) list and the Chair of the CVE Editorial Board. His operational experience is in vulnerability scanning and incident response. His research interests include automated vulnerability analysis of source code, reverse engineering of malicious executable code, and responsible vulnerability disclosure practices. He is a Principal INFOSEC Engineer in MITRE's Security and Information Operations Division. He holds a B.S. in Computer Science from Hobart College.

Position Statement 16

Paper entitled "Software Security" by Gary McGraw published in IEEE Computer Society, IEEE Security and Privacy, March/April 2004.

Dr. Gary McGraw
CTO, Cigital
"Gary McGraw" gem@cigital.com

Gary McGraw, Cigital, Inc.'s CTO, researches software security and sets technical vision in the area of Software Quality Management. Dr. McGraw is co-author of five best selling books: Exploiting Software (Addison-Wesley, 2004), Building Secure Software (Addison-Wesley, 2001), Software Fault Injection (Wiley 1998), Securing Java (Wiley, 1999), and Java Security (Wiley, 1996). A noted authority on software and application security, Dr. McGraw consults with major software producers and consumers. Dr. McGraw has written over sixty peer-reviewed technical publications and functions as principal investigator on grants from Air Force Research Labs, DARPA, National Science Foundation, and NIST's Advanced Technology Program. He serves on Advisory Boards of Authentica, Counterpane, and Fortify Software, as well as advising the CS Department at UC Davis. Dr. McGraw holds a dual PhD in Cognitive Science and Computer Science from Indiana University and a BA in Philosophy from UVa. He writes a monthly security column for Network magazine, is the editor of Building Security In for IEEE Security & Privacy magazine, and is often quoted in national press articles.

Position Statement 17

Many enterprises have invested in infra-structure for managing user identities and credentials as well as systems for providing access control to web applications. However, criteria for evaluating the quality of such systems as well as tools and tests that can investigate and report on these criteria have not been available. As a result, many enterprises only learn about weaknesses of their IAM systems after they have been hacked.

Principal Identity is developing a checklist of criteria relevant to IAM infrastructure. A set of tools (IAMscan) for analyzing enterprise infrastructure are also under development.

Prateek Mishra
CTO,Principal identity
<pmishra@principalidentity.com>

Prateek Mishra is CTO with a startup called Principal identity and we are creating some innovative security tools in the identity and access control space.

Position Statement 18

Detecting security issues in software source code is not dissimilar from the problem of detecting software defects through source analysis. Both problems are "NP hard" in the general case, but at the same time offer tremendous benefit for even partial solutions.

An interesting approach to both problems is to shift the focus from the absolute detection of the security issue or defect, to the identification of risk, by source code analysis combined with other data sources. By combining many different analyses and metrics of the source with statistical analysis engines, tools may identify the areas of the source code most likely to have defects and security issues, if indeed they exist.

James W. Nash
Nash Laboratories, Inc.
jwn@.nashlabs.com

Solidware Technologies (www.solidwaretechnologies.com) is an emerging company specializing in tools to manage software verification, validation, and risk. James W. Nash is a Principal with Solidware, and has been an active software developer, manager, and executive for more than 25 years. Nash received a BS in Computer Science from Michigan State University, and was certified as a Six Sigma Master Black Belt by the General Electric Company. Nash holds current certifications as a CMMI Lead Appraiser and Instructor from the Software Engineering Institute at Carnegie-Mellon, an as a Software Quality Engineer from the American Society for Quality.

Position Statement 19

My interest in NIST's workshop on "Defining the State of the Art in Software Security Tools" is threefold:

1. As the Executive Vice President of the Center for National Software Studies (CNSS), I am involved in "Software 2015: A National Software Strategy to Ensure U.S. Security and Competitiveness" designed to achieve the goal of being able to routinely develop and deploy trustworthy software products and systems by the year 2015 while ensuring the continued competitiveness of the U.S. software industry. One of its four programs calls for improving software trustworthiness, and one of the initiatives in achieving this is to develop measurement methods for a National Software Quality Index (NSQI). The report can be found at http://www.CNsoftware.org

2. In collaboration with the Council on Competitiveness, the CNSS conducted a workshop on "Competitiveness and Security". The knowledge required in this trade off revolves around the practices and factors that embrace both competitiveness and security and those that embrace one at the expense of the other. Three types of practices and factors are used to frame the issue including trustworthiness, cost effectiveness, and survivability. Leading indicators are identified for each practice. A web-based scoring and analysis tool is used to analyze the impact of trustworthiness, cost effectiveness, and survivability practices and factors on competitiveness and security. While both are essential, it is clear that competitiveness and security travel on separate paths that do crisscross and overlap at certain points. The competitiveness versus security trade off may be tilted towards competitiveness, thereby, exposing the national's critical software infrastructure to predictable security threats. My contribution to the workshop is the "Competitiveness Versus Security Tradeoff" fully discussed at http://members.aol.com/ONeillDon2/competitor5-6.html

3. As an Independent Consultant and director of the National Software Quality Experiment (NSQE), I have shared NSQE results with NIST's HISSA project which continues to link to them from the NIST web site. The centerpiece of the experiment is the Software Inspection Lab where data collection procedures, product checklists, and participant behaviors are packaged for operational project use. The uniform application of the experiment and the collection of consistent measurements are guaranteed through rigorous training of each participant. Thousands of participants from dozens of organizations are populating the experiment database with thousands of defects of all types along with pertinent information needed to pinpoint their root causes. The measurements taken in the lab and the derived metrics are organized along several dimensions including year, software process maturity level, organization type, product type, programming language, global region, and industry type. The NSQE results can be viewed at http://members.aol.com/ONeillDon/nsqe-results.html

Don O'Neill
Executive Vice President, Center for National Software Studies (CNSS)
OneillDon@aol.com

O'Neill is an independent consultant and Executive Vice President of the Center for National Software Studies (CNSS). He is also the director of the National Software Quality Experiment (NSQE).

Position Statement 20

Penetration testers routinely use attack graphs to help them understand a network's weaknesses. Roughly speaking, attack graph nodes represent network states, and attack graph edges represent the application of an exploit that transforms one network state into another, more compromised, network state. The terminal state of the attack graph represents a network state in which the attacker has achieved his or her goal. At the research level, methods have been proposed to construct attack graphs based on data provided by commercial vulnerability scanning tools. The salient observation is that attack graphs quickly become unmanageably large as network complexity grows past a few machines. One way out of this computational quagmire is to go back to the penetration tester's perspective and ask what structure short of the entire attack graph would nonetheless be useful. The answer is that penetration testers often think in terms of the maximal level of penetration possible with respect to a given host, and push the details of how to achieve this level to the background.

Our approach only retains the highest level of access that can be achieved between hosts. This allows our model to scale better than complete attack graphs in realistic size networks. This is because our host–centric model grows polynomially with the number of hosts, but the attack graph model grows exponentially. The approach can be used to provide near real–time early warning of potential attacks, to identify the network policy rules violations, and to conduct analysis on the potential impacts of giving different permissions or credentials to users (i.e., modeling insider attacks).

A working prototype tool has been implemented. It constructs an access graph with a node for each host. A directed edge from h1 to h2 in the access graph represents the access available on h2 from h1. The model to construct such a graph consists of two steps: 1) initialization and 2) calculating maximal level of access. The goal of initialization is to establish the initial trust relationships between hosts in absence of applying any exploits (obtained from existing trust relationships from network rules and configuration). The maximal level access is then calculated between all the hosts in the network by using each host's known exploits.

We have put together a companion website which describes our tool's usage by walking the reader through an example. It shows the tool's screenshots at different stages of access graph construction and analysis. The website address is: http://ise.gmu.edu/_jpamula/nist-workshop/host-based.html. To further demonstrate that our approach runs in reasonable time for realistic networks, we ran our tool on a network comprised of 87 hosts. The experiment was conducted on an Intel Pentium 4 (2.0 GHz) with 512 MBytes of RAM running on Fedora Core 3 (Linux 2.6.9). In our approach, there are as many nodes, as there are hosts in the network. Each host pair is analyzed, hence making $87^2 = 7569$ edges in the resulting access graph. Out of these edges, 2088 had level of access higher than connectivity. The open source graph visualization program, graphviz, was used to generate graphs for closer analysis and visualization. Before populating the system with existing trust relationships, the system first needs to be initialized with the network's topology/configuration. The tool reads-in this information from couple of files: "H.txt"—set of host nodes, "T.txt"—set of trust relationships between hosts, "X.txt"—set of available network exploits, "V.txt"—set of vulnerabilities present at each host in the network, and "F.txt"—set of firewall rules. This took 1.527 seconds to complete. To establish the initial trust relationships between hosts in absence of applying any exploits took 0.107 seconds. Then, 1.571 seconds took to calculate maximal accesses between all the hosts in the network using each host's known exploits. The graphviz tool was then used to generate access graph for visualization and analysis purposes.

Joseph Pamula
Student and Research Assistant at George Mason University
jpamula@gmu.edu

Joseph Pamula is a PhD student and a member of Center for Secure Information systems group at George Mason University. His current research interests include vulnerability analysis, penetration testing, intrusion detection, and network security. Joseph Pamula received his B.Sc. in Computer Science with honors from McGill University, Canada, in 2001. Contact him at jpamula@gmu.edu.

Position Statement 21

There is significant interest in tools for finding software defects, particularly defects that pose security vulnerabilities. Developing a set of metrics and reference benchmarks for evaluating such tools will be a difficult process. There is already substantial academic interest in developing software defect benchmarks for academic research (see the Workshop on Software Defect Detection Tools). One important goal for the NIST workshop should be to ensure that whatever benchmark, licensing terms and frameworks are developed are suitable for academic research and do not duplicate effort in the academic community. A particular problem is that many of the companies selling commercial defect detection tools now consider the abilities of their tools trade secrets. While companies such as Coverity used to post detailed listings of the warnings they generated on open source software, they no longer do so since they believe it gives their competitors a commercial advantage. This is a real business concern for these companies, and solutions will need to be found. However, any solution that prevents an open analysis by academic researchers of defects found or not found by various tools will hamper research in this area and be detrimental to the long term progress of the field. Another issue is that any attempt to develop a standard fixed set of benchmarks will, over the long term, do more harm that good. A fixed set of benchmarks will lead to companies focusing on those benchmarks rather than the problems that people are actually encountering. What we need is something much closer to the TREC (Text Retrieval Conference) competitions, where each year there is a new benchmark.

William Worthington Pugh Junior
 Dept. of Computer Science, University of Maryland, College Park, MD 20742
pugh@cs.umd.edu

Professor William Pugh's current major research area involves software defect tools for Java. He is a lead contributor to the FindBugs project, an open source static defect tool for Java; FindBugs has been downloaded more than 100,000 times from SourceForge. Professor Pugh was also a co-chair of the 2005 ACM SIGPLAN Workshop on Software Defect Detection Tools. He has also conducted research on concurrency, detection of near-duplicate web pages, Java classfile compression and loading and analysis of scientific programs for execution on supercomputers.

Position Statement 22

When I think of the current state-of-the-art of security analysis tools, I think of the following statement that I made over a decade ago when assessing testing tools "a fool with a tool is still a fool." Tools provide you limited information if you don't have a framework for using it. For the past four years, we have been trying to fill this void especially in the field of applications security where we have been developing tools and techniques to cope with software piracy, tampering and reverse engineering. The framework that we developed under SBIR Phase I contract W9113M-04-P-0122 is risk based. It identifies 34 categories of attack and 28 defense methods, some of which have been automated via tools. As part of the effort we have developed simple models for risk assessment and performed a preliminary gap analysis. Should we be invited to the workshop, we will share the results of this analysis with the community. Hopefully, it will serve as one of the pillars that DOD, NBS, NFS and other sponsors will use to perform their tools analysis.

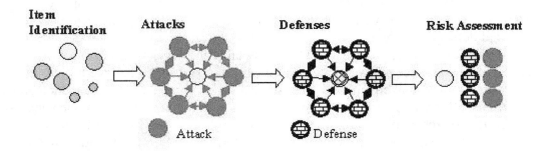

Donald J. Reifer, President
Reifer Consultants, Inc.
d.reifer@ieee.org

Donald J. Reifer is one of the leading figures in the field of software engineering and management with over thirty-five years of progressive experience in the field. Mr. Reifer has been a successful businessman, entrepreneur, software management consultant, government official, author and teacher. During the past eight years, he has focused his energy on software protection issues. He developed innovative algorithms for real-time response to intrusions that has been adopted for use within intrusion detection systems and holds a patent on "a method to protect applications software from reverse engineering and tampering." He has published five books and over one hundred papers including several dealing with malicious code protection. He holds many awards and prizes including the Secretary of Defense's Medal for Outstanding Public Service, the NASA Exceptional Service Medal, the Frieman Award and the AIAA Software Engineering Award.

Position Statement 23

While "attackers do not attack abstractions", much of what ensures a software system has the emergent security properties required occurs before coding in the establishment of security requirements, creation of a formal security policy, specification of external behavior, and design - plus the creation of the assurance arguments that they are consistent and functionality does not exceed specifications. According to one report, during one period half the security vulnerabilities discovered by Microsoft were the result of design (including, one presumes, bad requirements' impacts on design).

While some are better than one might expect, tools in this area need considerable improvement. The enabling technologies available in theorem provers such as PVS and model checkers such as SPIN are actually in many ways quite powerful. Combinations of such enabling technology with specification or design notations exist with Z (e.g. Z/EVES), CSP (e.g. FDR), and UML including formal notations (e.g. in the work of Jan Jurgens). These, however, often do not use the most powerful enabling technology available.

As users of such tools, we find them quite useful but with significant shortcomings. Many are under funded or research vehicles. This state of affairs is, of course, in part a function of low usage. Experts also seem to have a surprising willing to put up with poor usability. This characteristic, however, is a barrier to wider usage.

Two areas where wider usage does exist are in verification of protocols and hardware. The hardware area appears to have examples of making tools so advanced they are simple with the details of formal analysis hidden from the user, a characteristic that greatly aids in achieving wide usage.

A more important barrier to wider usage is the lack of awareness, skill, and readiness in the workforce and their management and customers. While the underlying mathematical knowledge needed by the user can be quite simple (e.g. in Z or model checkers), for most obtaining the proper mindset and skill in usage requires serious effort. On the other hand, we need to through good design, automation, and other means find ways for fewer (and better) people to be writing software where security is relevant.

The use of formal methods has been more extensive in systems where safety was a primary concern than where security was the driver. In safety the assurance argument is a central issue and artifact. The same must be true in security. The system must not only be secure, but one must have evidence justifying confidence this is so, and tools are needed to facilitate this.

Reference
Redwine, Samuel T., Jr., and Noopur Davis (Editors). Processes for Producing Secure Software: Towards Secure Software. Volumes I and II. Washington D.C.: National Cyber Security Partnership, 2004.

Samuel Redwine
James Madison University
redwinst@CISAT.JMU.EDU

An Associate Professor of Computer Science at James Madison University, Samuel T. Redwine, Jr. was lead editor of recent National Cyber Security Partnership's *Processes for Producing Secure Software*. He is General Chair of the upcoming Workshop on Secure Software Engineering Education and Training and the IEEE International Symposium on Secure Software Engineering. He is leading the DHS/DoD Software Assurance Initiatives' effort to produce a body of knowledge description for the knowledge required to produce secure software. Mr. Redwine has worked in industry and consulting for more than 30 years including time at Mitre, Institute for Defense Analyses, and the Software Productivity Consortium and been an Adjunct Professor at George Mason University and Virginia Tech. He has B. S. and M. S. degrees from M. I. T. and is a member of IEEE, ACM, and the American Society for Quality (ASQ). He is a former ASQ Certified Software Quality Engineer. Mr. Redwine has been a Distinguished Visiting Speaker for the IEEE Computer Society.

Position Statement 24

(Position Statement not received).

William Stanton Spees
USA CDRH (FDA)
wss@cdrh.fda.gov

I have been a developer of compilers and interpreters for twenty-five years, and am interested in exploring classes of security weaknesses that I might be able to avoid generating. I also develop ad hoc metric tools, occasionally and would be curious about conventional techniques by which they might be able to spot flaws.

After working in C and C++ from the 1970s until 1999, I am 100% pure Java. I finished my computer science Ph.D. in 2001, and have worked as a software consultant, college professor, and medical instrument software developer before joining the Center for Devices and Radiological Health (FDA) as a Senior Staff Fellow, earlier this year.

Position Statement 25

I am working with Mike Kass and Paul Black to leverage a project that we (National Security Agency (NSA) are conducting with the work being conducted under SAMATE. In discussions with Mike and Paul, we are considering having NIST focus on source code analysis tools and NSA focus on binary analysis tools. We have also discussed with them the leveraging/development of a reference set of software for test purposes. As I am working on the same types of problems (all areas of the workshop) for DoD, I look forward to this workshop.

Larry Don Wagoner
DOD
"Wagoner, Larry D." l.wagone@radium.ncsc.mil

I am working as the Information Assurance Directorate Technical Lead for Software Assurance at NSA and the co-leader of the Science and Technology Bin as part of the DoD Tiger Team for Software Assurance. I have worked in the area of vulnerability discovery and software analysis for many years.

Position Statement 26

1) Tools are useful to identify potential vulnerabilities quickly. However, false positives can have a negative impact and waste time.
2) It's unclear how to select the best tool with the least amount of false positives without using in the field.
3) Source code analysis is a more efficient means of detecting root causes. SCA tools are beneficial.
4) The costs of SCA tools can make them prohibitive for most assessment efforts.
5) Use of SCA tools in the development process by developers is optimal for minimizing vulnerabilities.

Stan Wisseman, CISP, CISM
Senior Associate, Booz | Allen | Hamilton
wisseman_stan@bah.com

1) 21 years in computer security.
2) I've led software security consulting practices for 3 years.

Position Statement 27

Static analysis tools are an important technology for the improvement of software security. They fill the role of an expert security code reviewer that never tires and performs accurately and repeatably. Most static analysis tools have taken the approach of analyzing source code, which requires the complete source code (including linked libraries) and an analyzer that can model the transformations a compiler makes accurately. A different static analysis approach that doesn't rely on having complete source code and looks at the compiler output directly is binary static analysis. Binary analysis' strength of complete program coverage and its analysis of the final executable makes it ideal for quality assurance testing, analyzing long completed legacy applications, and the acceptance testing of purchased code.

As part the development lifecycle, source and binary static analyzers are complementary security technologies. Fast, intraprocedural static analysis can be built into compilers that process one source file at a time. This approach catches insecure coding at the earliest point in the development cycle and gives immediate feedback to the developer. Binary analysis' deeper, interprocedural, whole program approach takes more modeling time. It can fit in at build time much like traditional automated testing does. Just as unit testing complements and doesn't replace final QA testing, source code analysis does not replace the need to perform a security analysis of the complete program executing the way it will when the program is in production.

Binary analysis' efficacy shines when it is difficult or impossible to obtain the complete source code for a program. Enterprise developers typically write a small percentage of a program's overall functional code. They produce business logic and use libraries for presentation, transaction processing, authorization, and database access. Binary analysis enables these developers to analyze the interaction of their source code with the libraries they use to understand the complete risk of a program. For legacy applications and purchased code, complete source code is not always available or easy to obtain. Binary analysis can give a view of a programs risk without a source code requirement.

There is a real need for organizations to understand the risks of deploying off-the-shelf applications they purchase. Riskier applications translate into a higher cost of ownership though increased patching and incident response costs. Organizations that can afford it conduct penetration testing, or hire security consultants to do it, as part their acceptance testing process prior to deploying new software. Binary analysis can bring the consistency and cost savings that static analysis brings to the development process to the acceptance testing process.

Chris Wysopal
Director, Development Symantec Corporation
cwysopal@gmail.com

I have been involved in software security research since the mid 90's. In 1996, as a security researcher at L0pht Heavy Industries, I published the first advisory for a vulnerability in a commercial web application, Lotus Domino. The advisory contains the first description of authorization bypass and session management problems in a web application. These are security issues that are still common today. I later published advisories on vulnerabilities I discovered in Microsoft IIS, Windows 95, NT and 2000. While at L0pht Heavy Industries I co-authored L0phtCrack, the first commercial Windows password auditor, and in 1998 I testified before the US Senate Committee on Governmental Affairs on the topic of "Weak Computer Security in Government".

In 1999, I co-founded @stake, a computer security research and consulting company that specialized in application security services. While consulting at Microsoft in 2002, I helped develop their threat modeling process, which is widely used throughout the industry today. I managed @stake's world class research team and @stake's process of working with vendors to disclose security vulnerabilities responsibly. In 2002, along with 10 other companies, I founded the Organization for Internet Safety, an organization dedicated to promoting guidelines for responsible vulnerability disclosure. In 2003, I testified before the US House of Representatives, Subcommittee on Technology, Information Policy, Intergovernmental Relations and the Census, on the topic of vulnerability research.

For the last 5 years at @stake (now Symantec), we have been researching the static analysis of binaries to find security flaws. We have developed technology that can take a binary compiled from C or C++ source code for Windows or Solaris and generate a list of security vulnerabilities. We have undergone comparisons with other static analyzers internally and at customer locations and have found our depth of analysis and false positive rate to be state of the art. I am interested in developing standards for the classes of application vulnerabilities that security tools test for and standardized metrics for quantifying the risk in applications.

Position Statement 28

As a security practitioner, I am actively involved in various aspects of software security in my consulting and training roles. Although I've been in the information security field for over 20 years, I've been particularly interested in software security for the past 5-7 years, as I've become increasingly disillusioned with the status quo, point solution (e.g., firewall, IDS, IPS, anti-virus...) attitudes that are so pervasive throughout the information security industry today.

Clearly, the security and software development communities need to pay far more than simple lip service to software security. Continuously improving the product solutions that are available to help software security professionals do their jobs more effectively is a vital aspect of that.

I eagerly welcome opportunities to better understand the software security product space and, to the extent that I am able to, help guide its future directions.

Kenneth R. van Wyk
Principal Consultant
ken@krvw.com

Kenneth R. van Wyk, CERT® Certified Computer Security Incident Handler, is an internationally recognized information security expert and author of the recent O'Reilly and Associates books, Incident Response and Secure Coding: Principles and Practices, as well as a monthly columnist for eSecurityPlanet. Ken is also a Visiting Scientist at the Software Engineering Institute of Carnegie Mellon University, where he is a course instructor and consultant to the CERT® Coordination Center.

Ken has previously held senior information security technologist roles at Tekmark's Technology Risk Management practice, Para-Protect Services, Inc., and Science Applications International Corporation (SAIC). Ken was also the Operations Chief for the U.S. Defense Information Systems Agency's DoD-CERT incident response team, as well as a founding employee of the CERT® Coordination Center at Carnegie Mellon University's Software Engineering Institute.

Ken has served as the Chairman and as a member of the Steering Committee for the Forum of Incident Response and Security Teams (FIRST) organization. He is a CERT® Certified Computer Security Incident Handler and holds an engineering degree from Lehigh University and is a frequent speaker at technical conferences, and has presented papers and speeches for CSI, ISF, USENIX, FIRST, and others.

Position Statement 29

In our research, a taxonomy is proposed for addressing the level of security in a networked-based system. The 3-A attributes of attacks, architecture, and administration are measured by a set of 7 easily obtainable tools. Using these measurements, a study was made of a small technological company, leading to the results that such tools are useful for uncovering hidden vulnerabilities, and that users are usually unaware of such vulnerabilities.

The security of a system is usually described in terms of the CIA attributes of security: Confidentiality (the ability to only allow those with a proper need to access information), Integrity (the ability to ensure that the information is not changed improperly), and Availability (the ability to ensure that the information is available when needed). Within a data communications network such as the Internet, this is achieved via four general processes:

1. Authentication - Ensuring that the user is the correct individual.

2. Authorization - Ensuring that the individual has the ability to access the necessary information.
3. Data integrity - Ensuring that the data has not been altered in some way.
4. Data privacy - Ensuring that the data has not been compromised or seen by others.

In our research we see security more effectively measured by our own taxonomy, which we call the AAA attributes of security:

1. Attacks. Attacks are the results of conscious attempts to break into a system. Intrusion detection systems (IDS) are software products (e.g., snort) that monitor a system's performance and indicate when outsiders are trying to infiltrate. Tools like tripwire determine if attacks have occurred. If attacks never occur, then there would be no need for security measures, much like the case in small towns where the risk of burglary is small. Doors often stay unlocked and yet little gets stolen.
2. Architecture. Architecture represents those features of a system that prevent successful attacks. Tools like Nessus use a database of over 1000 known vulnerabilities (e.g., the CVE library) to see if any of those vulnerabilities are present in a given system.
3. Administration. A major source of insecurity is the administration of a computer system. Using weak passwords or no password is a major cause of intrusions. Not protecting files, sharing files or running services like ftp servers without proper configuration are another source of vulnerability.

Therefore, if we want to measure the degree of security, or conversely, the risk of a successful attack, we have to monitor and measure these three attributes of attacks, architecture, and administration so that appropriate measures can be taken in order to make networked computer systems more predictable and less vulnerable to attacks.

We ran a small case study of 13 machines at the Fraunhofer Center Maryland (FC-MD) to see if we could identify vulnerabilities. We chose 7 inexpensive or free tools to measure the AAA attributes: Snort, NeWT (Nessus for Windows), Norton Anti-Virus software, FPort for checking open ports, Ad-Aware for malicious browser plugins, Microsoft Security Base Analyzer for detecting missing software updates and a manual check on specific registry entries looking for malicious programs. Our preliminary AAA measurement model so far is (Attacks [Snort], Architecture [MBSA], Administration [Norton, Ad-Aware, Registry, FPorts]) where X[Y] indicates that Y is a measure of attribute X.

Some preliminary results of our study are:
- Malicious applications in the start-up process of the machines. Most of the applications that were in the start-up keys of the registry were superfluous. Even though they don't cause any damage to the system, they can impede performance of the computer. When asked about the applications installed, most users didn't know about most of these. In addition, the set of applications on start-up registry keys related to software and hardware vendors was not the same in all machines,

even though they were running roughly the same hardware and software applications.

- When we looked at the ports that were open at a given time in each of the machines, the running processes were not malicious. Even though these applications are not necessarily dangerous we identified a need to educate users not to accept file transfer from untrustworthy sources. Another problem is that users use different types of instant messengers and rarely do they update their software; therefore, existing flaws in older versions can be exploited.
- NeWT identified several problems. NeWT classifies issues as note, info or hole. Note and info indicate situations that may be sources of exploitations, but are not problems in and of themselves. Systems administrators should be aware of them.

Even though we found several additional problems in these machines, FC-MD has a firewall that protects the network so many of the problems we uncovered, while potentially harmful, were benign The main concern is traffic that is initiated from the machines to the outside Internet, for example from plugins, and other tools used by users like instant messengers.

It is clear most people are unaware of all that is running on their machines and worse, it is not easy to find out. The tools we used were helpful, but still requires much knowledge about security to understand its results and what actions to take. We understood that the reason the configuration of the machines were so different was mainly due to different behavior of the different users. Understanding the different types of users is an important issue to figure out the appropriate security measures that are needed to protect a computer network.

Our preliminary case study had the following general conclusions:

1. Being behind a firewall has probably saved FC-MD from security problems, but we know that a firewall is not totally secure, so additional steps to minimize future problems need to be taken.
2. Two of the 13 machines studied were laptops. Laptops proved harder to keep up to date since they were disconnected from the network for long periods of time and were not automatically updated.
3. It is unclear why every machine, all used in a similar way, have such different configurations when they reboot (e.g., vastly different startup registry entries).

From our feasibility study, it is clear that users need a measurement plan that takes into account their security vulnerabilities beyond those of the relatively common email virus scanner so that they can understand how (in)secure they are. The fact that the configuration of the machines was so different led us to believe that the user behavior is an important variable in the measurement of security. Identifying what users can be expected to understand concerning security and how their behavior makes a vulnerability more or less dangerous can be an important factor to take into account when establishing a security policy for a computer network.

Marvin Zelkowitz
Department of Computer Science, University of Maryland and
Fraunhofer Center for Experimental Software Engineering, MD
marv@zelkowitz.com

Patricia Costa
Fraunhofer Center for Experimental Software Engineering,
pcosta@fc-md.umd.edu

Marvin Zelkowitz is a professor of Computer Science at the University of Maryland, College Park, Maryland since 1971 and is Chief Scientist of the Fraunhofer Center Maryland, which he joined in 1998. Previously he had a part-time faculty appointment with the Information Technology Laboratory (and its predecessors) of NIST from 1976 through 1997. His research interest is technology transfer, emphasizing experimental validation of new software technology.

Patricia Costa has been a scientist with the Fraunhofer Center Maryland, since 2000. She has a masters degree in Computer Science and a masters degree in Telecommunications Management.

Discussion Material

Here is discussion material that was developed by the NIST employees as starting points for discussion. These are rough drafts, preliminary versions, or sketches of the following to help generate discussion and comment:

- survey of SA security tools by categories,
- the state of the art in SA security tools,
- classes of software security flaws and vulnerabilities,
- possible metrics to evaluate SA security tools, and
- reference dataset.

Survey of SA Tools by Categories

Disclaimer

Any commercial product mentioned is for information only; it does not imply recommendation or endorsement by NIST nor does it imply that the products mentioned are necessarily the best available for the purpose.

This survey gathers information on tools and companies from web search engines, research papers, and product assessment reports. This initial list of tools and companies reflect a preliminary examination of the tool and its major types. The collection of tools is created and maintained in a database at NIST. Only a few tools have been obtained for hands-on investigation and executed with the reference dataset. We welcome contributions to add, delete, or modify the list.

Introduction

In order to survey the types of tools the SAMATE project is interested in, we must first distinguish between software quality versus software security assurance. In a simplified way, they are defined as follows:

- . *Software Quality Assurance* tools help developers produce quality software
- *Software Security Assurance* tools help detect flaws anywhere in the software development lifecycle that lead to security vulnerabilities.

This survey gathers information on software security assurance tools and companies from web search engines, research papers, and product assessment reports. This initial list of tools and companies reflects a preliminary examination of the tool and its major types. This information is maintained in a database at NIST. Only a few tools have been obtained for hands-on investigation and examined.

Discussion Points

There are many software assurance (SA) tools in the market place. Some are commercially available, others are open source. Some tools are designed to be used during particular system development life cycle. Tools also support varieties of features. The purpose of the tool survey is to help answer the following questions:

- What are the common features among tools of the same type?
- Where are the gaps in capabilities among the same types of tools?
- How would someone purchasing a tool know which one is the right one for their level of software security assurance?
- Should tools provide some kind of "assurance label" to their product that define what their tool can and cannot do?
- What might an "assurance label" look like (for example, on the back of a source code scanner software package)?

Classifying Tools

There are many ways to classify software assurance tools. One classification is "where" in the software development life cycle the tool is used:

- Requirements capture, design, specification tools
- Software design/modeling verification tools
- Implementation or production testing tools
- Operational testing tools

In an effort to scope the project, and due to limited resources, our survey focuses on SA tools used during software implementation and production.

Some tools specialize in identifying vulnerabilities within a specific type of application. The taxonomy used for this survey of SA tools is taken from Defense Information Systems Agency's (DISA) "Application Security Assessment Tool Market Survey," Version 3.0, July 29, 2004 [1]. This taxonomy is also used to identify SA functions. See discussion material "The State of the Art in SA Tools and Their Functions."

Web Application Tools: Web application scanner tools are a more specialized class of SA tool that focuses specifically on web applications only, and are not considered generalized network scanners.

Examples of this type of tool and company are as:

- AppScan DE by Watchfire, Inc.
- N-Stealth by N-Stalker
- NTOSpider by NTObjectives
- Spike Proxy by Immunity
- TestMaker by pushtotest

- WebScarab by OWASP

Web Service Tools: Web service scanner tools are a relatively new class of SA tool whose purpose is the analysis of web service applications.

Examples of this type of tool and company include:

- SOAPscope by Mindreef
- SOA Test by Parasoft

Database Tools : Database Scanner tools are a specialized tool used specifically to identify vulnerabilities in database applications. In addition to performing some "external" functions like "password cracking", the tools also examine the internal configuration of the database for possible exploitable vulnerabilities.

Examples of this type of tool and company include:

- AppDetective by Application Security Inc.

Developer Tools: Developer tools are used to identify software vulnerability during development or after deployment. This is the main focus of the SAMATE project. These tools consist of static source code analysis tool, disassembler debugger decompiler, binary code/byte code analysis tool, and dynamic run-time analysis tools.

Examples of Static Source Code Analysis Tools include*:*

- BOON by D. Wagner
- BoundsChecker, Dev Partner by Compuware
- Code Assure by Secure Software Inc.
- CodeSurfer, CodeSonar by GrammaTech, Inc.
- Eau Claire by Brian Chess
- Prevent/Extend by Coverity
- Cqual by Jeff Foster
- Flawfinder by David Wheeler
- Fortify Source Code Analysis by Fortify
- ITS4 by Cigital
- K7 by Klocworks
- Jtest by Parasoft
- PolySpace by PolySpace Technologies
- Prexis by Ounce Labs, Inc.
- RATS by Secure Software
- RSM Source code by Msquared Technologies
- Splint by U. of Virginia
- SPIdynamics
- Jlint by Artho.com
- PMD by InfoEther, Inc.

- UNO by Bell Labs
- xg++ by Stanford

Examples of Disassembler, Debugger, Decompiler tools include:

- IDA PRO by DataRescue Inc.
- VmWare Vitual Infrastructure by VmWare
- Boomerang by Boomerang Open Source Community Project
- Hindsight by Virtutech
- Fakebust by Michal Zalewski

Examples of Binary/Bytecode Analyzer include:

- AspectCheck by Aspect Security
- FindBugs by University of Maryland
- BugScan by LogicLab
- BEAST Binary Executable Analysis by Security Innovation
- Object Code Buffer Overflow Engine (OBOE) by ZelTech

Examples of Dynamic Analysis tools include:

- Holodeck by Security Innovation
- Rational Purify by IBM

General Purpose and Network Security Tools: - These tools scan networks and systems for potential security weaknesses and recommend fixes. Examples of this type of tool include:

- NESSUS by Tenable Security
- ELLIOTT by Open Source
- Enterprise Security Manager by Symantec
- Foundstone Professional TL by Found Stone
- Vulnerability Manager by NetIQ

The above listed are obtained from references and we welcome any additions, deletions or modifications.

Reference:
[1] Defense Information Systems Agency, "Application Security Assessment Tool Market Survey," Version 3.0, July 29, 2004.
[2] Concurrent Technology Corporation, "Code Assessment Methodology Project, Software Selection Report," Version 1.1, Prepared for: Maryland Procurement Office MDA904-03-C-1107, May 27, 2005
[3] Arian J. Evans, "Tools of the Trade: AppSec Assessment Tools" Presentation viewgraph from OWASP AppSec Europe 2005.

[4] Freeland Abbott and Joseph Saur, "Product Evaluation Report: A Comparison of Code Checker Technologies for Software Vulnerability Evaluation," Joint Systems Integration Command Report, 25 April 2005 (limited distribution for official use only).
[5] Jos Azario, "Source Code Scanners for Better Code," in Linux Journal. http://www.linuxjournal.com/article/5673.

The State of the Art in SA Tools and their Functions

Introduction

A definition of Software Assurance (SA) is: ... the planned and systematic set of activities that ensures that software processes and products conform to requirements, standards, and procedures. As defined by NASA [2]. Inherent in that definition is the assurance that products conform to software security requirements, standards and procedures. One of the goals of the SAMATE project is to determine the start of the art in software security tools that assist in assuring security compliance.

In order to begin this process, a taxonomy of SA tool classes and their functions is needed. The taxonomy below is a start at defining tool classes and functions. It is a hierarchical taxonomy, based upon the types of tools used at the various points in the software development lifecycle (SLDC). Much of the information used to construct this taxonomy is taken from Defense Information Systems Agency;s (DISA) Application Security Assessment Tool Market Survey, a document whose content will be posted publicly as a Security Techical Implementation Guide (STIG). Additionally, Secure Software Inc.'s CLASP v1.1 Training Manual provided much of the information for the proposed functional taxonomy of static code analysis tools.

Questions that need to be answered in order to complete the SA Tool/Function taxonomy include:

Regarding Tool Classes

- What classes of tools are currently used to identify potential vulnerabilities in applications today?
- What is the order of importance of those tools (which have the highest impact in of identifying/preventing application vulnerabilities)?
- What tool classes are most mature?
- What tool classes are most common?
- What are the gaps in capabilities amongst tools of the same class?
- What are the gaps in capabilities for a tool class in general?
- What classes of tools are missing from the taxonomy of SA tools below?

Regarding Tool Functions

- What are the functions that define a particular tool class?
- What functions are essential/required for a particular class of tool?
- What is the domain for each function?
- How would each function be described in a functional specification for that SA tool?
- What functions are missing from the taxonomy of SA tools below?

A Taxonomy of Tools and Functions

The taxonomy below is "hierarchical" in the sense that tools are classified as either "external" or "internal". External tools do not have access to application software code and/or configuration and audit data (such as network scanners or black-box testing tools). Internal tools (such as system, source code or binary code scanners) do. Additionally, some tools can be classified as both internal and external. An example of a possible SA tool taxonomy is: (much of the taxonomy content is borrowed from DISA [3], Secure Software [4] and NASA [5]).

External

- Network Scanners
- Web Application Scanners
- Web Services Network Scanners
- Dynamic Analysis Tools

Internal

- Software Requirements Verification Tools
- Software Design/Modeling Verification Tools
- Source Code Scanning Tools
- Byte Code Scanning Tools
- Binary Code Scanning Tools

Both Internal/External

- Database Scanning Tools
- General Network/System Security Scanners

References

[1] Defense Information Systems Agency, Application Security Assessment Tool Market Survey, Version 3.0, July 29, 2004.
[2] http://satc.gsfc.nasa.gov/assure/assurepage.html Software Assurance Guidebook and Standard page (17 Nov 2004).

[3] DISA Application Security Assessment Tool Survey, V3.0, July 29, 2004 (to be published as a STIG).
[4] http://www.securesoftware.com/solutions/clasp.html , CLASP Reference Guide, Volume 1.1 Training Manual, John Viega, Secure Software Inc., 2005.
[5] http://satc.gsfc.nasa.gov/tools/index.html Home page for the NASA Automated Requirement Measurement Tool.

Classes of Software Security Flaws and Vulnerabilities

- *Software security flaws* - software defects, inadvertently or intentionally introduced, that violate the desired security properties of a computer or network system, such as confidentiality, integrity and availability.
- *Vulnerabilities* - flaws in a software product that can be exploited to compromise the security of computer or network system.

Motivation for Classes of Software Security Flaws & Vulnerabilities

- *For Systematic Study* – classify security problems in software into categories that one can dissect for systematic study.
- *For SSA Tools Developing* - a taxonomy of security vulnerability that the SA community would agree upon will be essential for evaluating Software Security Assurance (SSA) tools and classifying SSA functions.
- *For SRD Developing* - Classes of software security flaws and vulnerabilities is one of resources to drive a standard reference dataset, which, in simply put, is a benchmark test suite for Software Security Assurance tools.

Characteristics of Satisfactory Taxonomies [1]

- mutually exclusive - classifying in one category excludes all others because categories do not overlap,
- exhaustive - taken together, the categories include all possibilities,
- unambiguous - clear and precise so that classification is not uncertain, regardless of who is classifying,
- accepted - logical and intuitive so that they could become generally approved,
- Useful - can be used to gain insight into the field of inquiry.

These characteristics can be used to evaluate possible taxonomies. It should be expected, however, for a satisfactory taxonomy to be limited in some of these characteristics. A taxonomy is an approximation of reality that is used to gain greater understanding in a field of study. Because it is an approximation, it will fall short in some characteristics.

[1] Edward G. Amoroso, *Fundamentals of Computer Security Technology*, Prentice-Hall PTR, Upper Saddle River, NJ, 1994.

Examples of Computer & Network Security Taxonomies

- List of Vulnerabilities
  - ➤ Frederick B. Cohen, *Protection and Security on the Information Superhighway*, John Wiley & Sons, New York, 1995.
- List of Categories of Vulnerabilities
  - ➤ William R. Cheswick and Steven M. Bellovin, *Firewalls and Internet Security: Repelling the Wily Hacker*, Addison-Wesley Publishing Company, Reading, MA, 1994.
- List of Categories of Results
  - ➤ Deborah Russell and G. T. Gangemi, Sr., *Computer Security Basics*, O'Reilly & Associates, Inc., Sebastopol, CA, 1991.
- Matrices
  - ➤ T. Perry and P. Wallich, "Can Computer Crime Be Stopped?," *IEEE Spectrum*, Vol. 21, No. 5.

	Operators	Programmers	Data Entry	Internal	Outside	Intruders
Physical Destruction	*Bombing Short circuits*					
Information Destruction	*Erasing Disks*	*Malicious software*			*Malicious software*	*Via modem*
Data Diddling		*Malicious software*	*False data entry*			
Theft of Services		*Theft as user*		*Unauthorized action*	*Via modem*	
Browsing	*Theft of media*			*Unauthorized access*	*Via modem*	
Theft of Information				*Unauthorized access*	*Via modem*	

- Tree Structure
  - ➤ Carl E. Landwehr, Alan R. Bull, John P. McDermott, and William S. Choi, "A Taxonomy of Computer Security Flaws," *ACM Computing Surveys*, Vol. 26, No. 3, September, 1994, pp. 211-254.

				Non-Replicating
			Trojan Horse	Replicating (virus)
		Malicious	Trapdoor	
	Intentional		Logic/Time Bomb	
				Storage
		Non-Malicious	Covert Channel	Timing
Genesis			Other	
		Validation Error (Incomplete/Inconsistent)		
		Domain Error (Including Object Re-use, Residuals, and Exposed Representation Errors)		
	Inadvertent	Serialization/aliasing		
		Identification/Authentication Inadequate		
		Boundary Condition Violation (Including Resource Exhaustion and Violable Constraint Errors)		
		Other Exploitable Logic Error		

- Multiple Dimensions
  - John Howard, "An Analysis of Security Incidents on the Internet 1989-1995," PhD dissertation in Engineering and Public Policy, Carnegie Mellon University, 1997.

Attackers	Tools	Access				Results	Objectives
Hackers	User Command	Implementation Vulnerability	Unauthorized Access		Files	Corruption of Information	Challenge, Status
Spies	Script or Program	Design Vulnerability	Unauthorized Use	Processes	Data in Transit	Disclosure of Information	Political Gain
Terrorists	Autonomous Agent	Configuration Vulnerability				Theft of Service	Financial Gain
Corporate Raiders	Toolkit					Denial-of-service	Damage
Professional Criminals	Distributed Tool						
Vandals	Data Tap						

  - Secure Software, Inc. "CLASP", 2005.
    - Three axes: Problem Type, Consequence, Exposure Period.

Possible Goals of Classifying Software Security Flaws & Vulnerabilities

- A taxonomy that has classification categories with the satisfactory characteristics as possible.
- Incorporate commonly used terms in security vulnerabilities that occurred in modern days.
- Consensus from the SA community.

Taxonomy Scope

- Including vulnerabilities in server applications and client applications, e.g. UNIX programs (sendmail, BIND, etc), server-type program (ftp, http, irc, finger, etc.), mail clients (MS Outlook, Netscape mail, etc.), COTS, etc.
- Not including vulnerabilities related to network, computer system environment, configuration, system design, system access validation, etc.
- Each class of vulnerability may have a collection of subclasses. Each subclass is a variation of the class. The whole collection of subclass does not intend to fully represent that class.
- Each attack may exhibit any combination of the vulnerability classes and/or subclasses.

Initial Draft

Input Validation Error

Input passed to an application is not properly validated such that vulnerability can be exploited by a certain input sequence.

Boundary Overflow

Input exceeds an assumed boundary thereby causing vulnerability. For example, the application may run out of memory, a variable might reach its maximum value and roll over to its minimum value, etc.

Buffer Overflow

A special case of Boundary Overflow, where the bounds checking on the size of input being stored in a buffer array is not performed or in error. This type of vulnerability comes with different flavors, include:

Upper/Lower Bound

Upper or lower bound is violated.

Data Type

Buffer of all data types (character, integer, floating point, wide character, pointer, unsigned character, and unsigned integer) may be overflowed. The attacker may use different technique for different data type to exploit the buffer overflow vulnerability.

Memory Location

Buffer may reside in different locations (stack, heap, data region, BSS, shared memory, etc.). The attacker may use different technique for different memory location to exploit the buffer overflow vulnerability.

Malformed Input

Input passed to a procedure call in an application is not properly checked such that vulnerability can be exploited by a certain input sequence.
Tainted Input to Call-Out Resources

Command Injection

Input passed to a command isn't properly sanitized before being used in a command execution call such as "system ()", "exec()" or "popen()". This can be exploited to inject arbitrary shell commands.

SQL Injection

Input passed to SQL query of an application, mostly found within webpages with dynamic content, isn't properly sanitized before being used. This can be exploited to cause computer security breach.

Format String

Hostile input passed as the format string for a variable arguments routine such as printf, the attacker can write arbitrary values to memory. The %n directive is particularly susceptible to attack.

Cross-Site Scripting

A web site may inadvertently include malicious HTML tags or script in a dynamically generated page based on unvalidated input from untrustworthy sources. This can be a problem when a web server does not adequately ensure that generated pages are properly encoded to prevent unintended execution of scripts, and when input is not validated to prevent malicious HTML from being presented to the user.

Directory Traversal

Directory traversal is an exploit that performs malicious activities such as accessing restricted directories, executing commands and viewing data outside the normal server directory where the application content is stored. Commonly, this vulnerability occurs when the web server software fails to validate input received from browsers.

Exceptional Condition Handling Error

The handling (or mishandling) of the exception by the application enables a vulnerability.

Symlink Problem

When temporary file being created insecurely, it can be exploited via symlink attacks to create and overwrite arbitrary files with the privileges of the user running the affected script.

Insecure Access Control – Application level
Access control mechanism is faulty; bad permission.

Privilege Escalations
Unauthorized users gain escalated privileges.

Improper Database Access
Database server improperly sets the access control for its clients. The client might be able to run arbitrary code on the server.

Cryptographic Error – Application level
Cryptographic service is faulty.

Random Number
A random number vulnerability occurs when a program uses a method of generating random numbers is predictable, e.g. rand(), random().

Race Conditions
A race condition occurs when multiple processes access and manipulate the same data concurrently, and the outcome of the execution depends on the particular order in which the access takes place. A race condition is of interest to a hacker when the race condition can be utilized to gain privileged system access.

Memory Leak
A flaw in a program that prevents it from freeing up memory that it no longer needs. As a result, the program grabs more and more memory until it finally crashes because there is no more memory left.

Null Pointer Dereference
Under some circumstances, a null pointer may be dereferenced during a memory allocation.

Backdoor/Input Sensitivity
Some specific input triggers malicious code.

Other
It is estimated that approximately 21% of CVE vulnerability entries are not classified.

Possible Metrics to Evaluate SA Security Tools

How can one determine that a tool does (or will do) what a user wants, in this case, find security vulnerabilities in programs? How can the strengths of different tools be assessed to determine which one or combination is good for what situation? This page has an initial draft of possible answers.

This also presents a initial list of features for code scanning tools. In the future, these features will be elaborated with testable assertions and a detailed test plan will be developed.

This page has an initial draft. One purpose of matter here is to be a starting point for discussion. Please read and consider this before the workshop. Be prepared to talk about your critiques, concerns, issues, suggestions, references, alternatives, etc.

Tool Metrics

Many of these metrics implicitly include the question of what dataset should be used. This question is addressed in the reference dataset. The ideas here come from many sources, for instance, the works of Abbott, Almazan, Foster, Kratkiewicz, Leek, Li, Lippmann, Lu, Qin, Rutar, Saur, Tan, Zhivich, Zhou, and Zitser. These metrics may not be very applicable to completely different classes of SA security tools, such as verifiers, requirements capture and validation tools, etc.

- Completeness

    Did the tool find everything, or more specifically, everything in the class of vulnerabilities it was designed for? Like "recall" in text retrieval.

    A common metric is number of correctly flagged vulnerabilities - total number of vulnerabilities.

    Called detection rate in, e.g., Kratkiewicz & Lippmann, and Zhivich, Leek, & Lippmann.

- Report Granularity

    How much information is given for each vulnerability flagged? Some kinds of information are:

    o Location of vulnerability

    Lu, et. al. call the space (for static analysis) or time (for dynamic analysis) between the occurrence and the flag the "detection latency".

    o Severity

o Class, vulnerability, or error

It is more helpful to say "buffer overflow at line 626" than just "line 626".

o Likelihood of really being a vulnerability

- Soundness

    Did the tool only report actual vulnerabilities, that is, no false alarms? Like "precision" in text retrieval.

    A common metric is number of false alarms / total number of vulnerabilities.

    Called false alarm rate in, e.g., Kratkiewicz & Lippmann, and Zhivich, Leek, & Lippmann.

- Scalability

    What is the growth in time or space for input size? This is used to give one indication of whether the tool can handle large pieces of software.

    A metric might be complexity (big-O notation), determined experimentally or by algorithm analysis. Another metric might be the size of the biggest piece of software it can handle (or has handled).

- Speed

    How fast is it? Complexity gives the shape of the curve, this gives the constants.

    For static analysis, this is the time taken. For dynamic analysis this is the start up or one shot analysis time and the execution slow down.

- Breadth

How widely can this be used?

    o What languages or binaries does it work with?
    o What platforms does it work on?

- Ease of Use Metrics

    These are often vital for specific determinations and have been used in surveys and comparisons. However, since these tend to be even more subjective than the above, we do not plan to consider them.

o Is a special set-up needed? For instance, special hardware.

o Ease of installation

o Updates & maintenance frequency and ease of updates

o Support and helpfulness of the vendor or developer

o Cost

o User learning time

o Annotation or preparation time. How much time does it take to prepare to a piece of software? Dynamic analysis may need test cases, if appropriate tests are not already available.

Reference Dataset

Goals

The purpose of the reference dataset is to provide researchers, developers, and consumers with a database of known bugs and vulnerabilities and fixes for them. This will allow developers to test their methods and consumers to evaluate a tool when considering it for purchase. The dataset should encompass a wide variety of possible vulnerabilities, languages, platforms, and compilers. We would like the dataset to become a large-scale effort, gathering examples from many sources.

Dataset Composition

How should the test suite cases be written? Should we construct artificial test cases to cover a wide range of exploits, or should test cases be sampled from "in the wild" source code? Would a mixture of multiple sources be most appropriate? What will provide more useful feedback?

Code Sources

"Artificial" Code
Constructing code samples that illustrate possible bugs and vulnerabilities would be one effective way of creating reference dataset. By selecting elements from a taxonomy of vulnerabilities, one could code examples and quickly produce a set that covers a wide range of bugs. Would performance on these "artificial" cases reflect a tools ability to perform on real code? How can we ensure that they are sufficiently complex? What are some effective methods for generating test cases without having to write them individually?

"Wild" Code

Sampling code from known bugs available in industry and open source software would allow us to construct a test set that encompasses real bugs that are found in software. By using the version of the code with the known vulnerability and comparing it to the "patched" version we can generate a correct and buggy example. Several studies have used open source software to compare error detection rates of leading SA tools. Is the size of the program prohibitive, and if so how much time is required to extract the buggy components and the corresponding fixed components? What licensing restrictions apply? Is it appropriate for the distribution of bugs in the test suite to correspond to the distribution of actual bugs found in software, or should more focus be put on covering as many types of bugs as possible? If we are only sampling from vulnerabilities that survived an internal debugging process, would they be valid for evaluating a tools ability to catch all bugs or simply the "hardest"?

"Academic" Code

Bill Pugh has constructed MARMOSET, a dataset consisting of code samples from introductory computer science courses at the University of Maryland. By sampling code from undergraduate course work, one is able to construct a large dataset of similar programs, which can be useful as a source of multiple correct and buggy programs. These could be extremely useful analyzing false positive, since they will provide many correct code samples that vary in structure. We must consider whether this code will provide an accurate means for evaluating SA tools. Are the errors and bugs introduced in undergraduate work the same as those in professionally produced software? Is the course work sufficiently complex to be used to evaluate tools that are intended for industry software? What range of concepts (threads, networking, cryptography, etc) does the course work cover compared to "real" software?

Code Size

What is an appropriate size for a test case? Should test cases be short and simple illustrate the vulnerability (i.e. an off-by-one index for a buffer), or should they be longer and more complex? Should the code be longer? How obfuscated should the bugs be? Would using whole application such as Mozilla or Apache be useful? What is reasonable or unreasonable for current tools?

Flawed and Fixed Samples

Our test suite should encompass a variety of flawed code, but also corresponding fixed code for each test case (that could be used to test false-positive rates). In most cases there will be many different possible solutions. How many different solutions would be appropriate? How complex should solutions be? Some solutions could fix the code, but in the process make it very convoluted. How complex/simple would solutions have to be? How should the fixed and buggy versions be linked to each other? If there are many different buggy versions and fixed versions should they all be linked together in the database?

Types of Vulnerabilities

What types of vulnerabilities should be selected? What languages should be the primary focus? What compilers, platforms, and applications (servers, browsers, etc) would be most useful for testing purposes? If a piece of code is buggy only on certain compilers, should it be included or should errors introduced by a compiler be ignored?

Dataset Structure

How should the reference dataset be stored and structured? What is an appropriate way to organize it and make it easily distributable?

Database Format

How should the reference dataset be stored and structured? What is an appropriate database system for storing and organizing this information? Should it be stored as an XML document or in a relational database? What are the strengths and weaknesses of each approach, and what would be easiest for the community to use?

Important Features

What are some important features that need to be present in the dataset? How should pieces of code be label and categorized? What metadata should be necessary for an entry in the dataset? The source of the code, the name of the person who discovered it, the language, platform and compiler all seem like necessary fields. A classification of the vulnerability, based on the taxonomy, also seems important, as well as an example of input that will exploit the vulnerability or cause buggy behavior. What are some other useful features for searching the database? LOC? cyclomatic complexity? keywords? other code metrics?

Maintenance

How should test cases be added and how should they be verified? Who should be authorized to add new elements? Who should be able to add new class of bugs as they are discovered? How can we efficiently distribute the reference dataset and its updates to companies, universities, and researchers? What are some appropriate methods for version control? Where should it be hosted and how should it be mirrored?

Workshop Minutes

This section contains the viewgraphs used by the facilitators followed by attributed and unattributed discussions which occurred during the workshop. Although we attempted to capture all the discussion points and correctly attribute them, the transcription provide failed to capture much information. So much points are missing. The views expressed by all participants are strictly their own and do not necessarily reflect those of their respective affiliated institutions, if any, nor the sponsors of this workshop.

Paul Black: Welcome to our workshop on the state of the art in software security tools. We originally expected about 25 to 30 people, but the response is overwhelming. We have Dr. Shashi Phoha, director of Information Technology Laboratory. She was head of the department at Penn State and research laboratories. So we are delighted to have Dr Phoha as the head of ITL at NIST.

Welcome (Shashi Phoha)

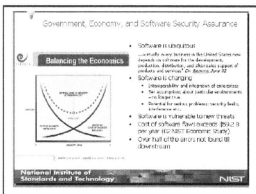

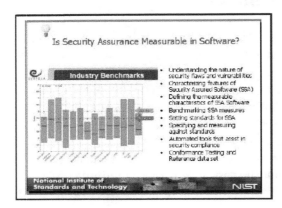 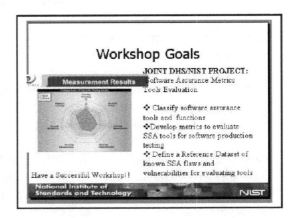

Shashi Phoha: I'm very pleased to be here. I believe very strongly that what you're doing here is the heart of our mission. I'll try to relate some of my views about this work. It is a very important area that we are dealing with. The goal of NIST is to create innovation so that machines can be compatible, to refacilitate trade, enhance safety, improve quality, and create jobs. I think this forum is living proof of how to do it and how to support the areas for today. The standards we have set enable me to concentrate on the message of scientific enquiry. Can we have more reliable systems? I believe that the answer is yes, and that this group can find it. There are many challenges; you're on the right track. You really have to understand the nature of security flaws and vulnerability and what features can be present in security flaws. You can identify certain features that will point out there is likely a security flaw. Then comes the automatic tools which must be present in making this happen. So I appreciate this inaugural workshop to a series sponsored by the Department of Homeland Security. The community has responded.

Scope and Introduction (Paul Black)

 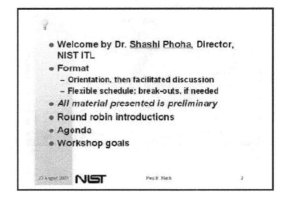

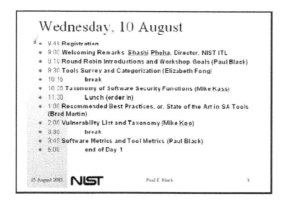

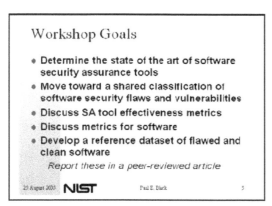

Paul Black: We appreciate your taking time out of your busy schedules to come and work hard. This workshop is going to be different: we're going to be talking with each other. Our format is going to be different. It's going to be an open discussion. We'll have several sessions where a facilitator is going to present the same discussion material which was on the web as orientation information, and then we'll have an open discussion. It will require cooperation on everyone's part. It's going to be a different experience.

Flexible agenda

Our agenda is going to be flexible. We will have an outline of an agenda which I think is reasonable, but if we find that one area is exhausted and no one has anything to say, we will just continue on.

Our agenda is more of a diagram. If we need to have a breakout session with 12-15 people about a critical issue that we want to discuss now, then we can do that! All the material that we present is preliminary. We have worked hard on it, but we are approaching this with not as much experience as most of you. Many of you have spent years in your field. So we are not saying this is the end-all be-all of the universe. This is material that we put together to be a basis. So please don't look at this and say, "It's no use - things are going to be the wrong way". These are preliminary ideas.

Round-robin introductions

Please state your name, what you represent and why you are here. (Introductions from everyone.)

Scope
"Security is not only code, it's also design, process, etc."

Paul E. Black: Scope of this workshop includes design, software development, the operating environment (OS, connections, services, libraries, etc.), and the operation. Software security tool effectiveness is one family of metrics. How much security do you get if you get it to comply with a certain tool? What sort of messages make sense to people about security, vulnerability, passwords, etc. Some people need the line of code. In additional to the proceedings, there will be a scientific article. Our goal for writing the article is about Mid-September.

Thoughts on the Reference Dataset

William Pugh: I see similarity to parallel computing back in the 90's. I saw the damage that was done to that field by inappropriate benchmarks. I'm happy that there were people, rather than trying to write to the benchmarks, that did a better job of getting parallelism.

John Barkley: I can refer to line 150 of the benchmark when establishing the tool necessary for reference data sets.

William Pugh: [Some benchmarks are] a lot of single dimensions where security is inherently multi-dimensional.

John Barkley: I think that's a very good point, there is no reason that the reference data has to be single dimensional. It could very well be multi-dimensional, indeed.

Brian Chess: My only concern about that is if you don't get benchmarks, some people will only do one thing very well and totally forget about the other stuff. We're looking at an upper level and a minimal level. Our challenge will always be to raise the bar.

William Pugh: I'm not saying there is nothing that can be done. You need to be careful. A benchmark may be bad because people have a tendency to build to the benchmark, even if that doesn't make real progress or even impedes progress.

John Barkley: They're constantly updated. We want to identify the main aspects of the reference datasets. People will run the same comparisons over and over, which will be useless. What you're trying to figure out is the best thing you can do.

Tools Survey and Categorization (Elizabeth Fong)

National Institute of Standards and Technology NIST

List of Software Security Tools by Categories

Elizabeth Fong
NIST

Disclaimer: Any commercial product mentioned is for information only; it does not imply recommendation or endorsement by NIST nor does it imply that the products mentioned are necessarily the best available for the purpose.

NIST National Institute of Standards and Technology • Technology Administration • U.S. Department of Commerce

---

Software Security Tools

- **Software Security Tools** help detect malicious and poor coding practices that lead to security vulnerabilities.

NIST National Institute of Standards and Technology • Technology Administration • U.S. Department of Commerce

---

Purpose of Survey

- To find out what kinds of Software Security Tools are available in the marketplace
- To find out what are the common features among tools of the same type
- To identify gaps in capabilities among the same type of tools

NIST National Institute of Standards and Technology • Technology Administration • U.S. Department of Commerce

---

Tools for a specific application set*

- Web Application Tools
- Database Tools
- Web Services Tools
- Developer Tools
- General Purpose Tools

* Defense Information Systems Agency, "Application Security Assessment Tool Market Survey," Version 3.0 July 29, 2004

NIST National Institute of Standards and Technology • Technology Administration • U.S. Department of Commerce

---

Tools Organized by Life Cycle Time

- Requirements capture, design, specification.
- Implementation or production
- Post-production/post-release
- Operation

NIST National Institute of Standards and Technology • Technology Administration • U.S. Department of Commerce

---

Tools Not Included in this Survey

- Unit tester or test generation tools
- Code coverage tools
- Compiler validation tools
- Code slicing tools

NIST National Institute of Standards and Technology • Technology Administration • U.S. Department of Commerce

Code Analysis Tools

- Static Source Code Scanner for C/C++
- Static Source Code Scanner for Java
- Binary Code Analysis
- Dynamic Run-Time Analysis

NIST National Institute of Standards and Technology • Technology Administration • U.S. Department of Commerce

Static Source Code Scanner

- BOON by D. Wagner
- BoundsChecker, Dev Partner by Compuware
- CodeAssure by Secure Software Inc.
- CodeSurfer, CodeSonar by GrammaTech, Inc.
- Eau Claire by Brian Chess
- Prevent/Extend by Coverity
- Cqual by Jeff Foster
- Flawfinder by David Wheeler
- Fortify Source Code Analysis by Fortify

NIST National Institute of Standards and Technology • Technology Administration • U.S. Department of Commerce

Static Source Code Scanner   (2)

- ITS4 by Cigital
- K7 by Klocworks
- Jlint by Cyrille Artho
- PolySpace by PolySpace Technologies
- Prexis by Ounce Labs, Inc.
- RATS by Secure Software
- RSM Source Code by M Squared Technologies
- Splint by U. of Virginia
- UNO
- xg++ by Stanford U.

NIST National Institute of Standards and Technology • Technology Administration • U.S. Department of Commerce

Disassembler Debugger Decompiler and Binary Code Analyzer

- IDA PRO by DataRescue Inc.
- VmWare Virtual Infrastructure by VmWare
- Boomerang by Boomerang Open Source Community Project
- Hindsight by Virtutech
- Fakebust by Michal Zalewski

NIST National Institute of Standards and Technology • Technology Administration • U.S. Department of Commerce

Binary Code/Bytecode Analyzer

- AspectCheck by Aspect Security
- FindBugs by U. of Maryland
- BugScan by LogicLab
- BEAST Binary Executable Analysis by Security Innovation
- Object Code Buffer Overflow Engine (OBOE) by ZelTech

NIST National Institute of Standards and Technology • Technology Administration • U.S. Department of Commerce

Dynamic Analyzer

- Holodeck by Security Innovation
- Rational Purify by IBM

NIST National Institute of Standards and Technology • Technology Administration • U.S. Department of Commerce

Web Application Tools*

- AppScan DE by Watchfire, Inc.
- N-Stealth by N-Stalker
- NTOSpider by NTObjectives
- Spike Proxy by Immunity
- TestMaker by Pushtotest
- WebScarab by OWASP

* Defense Information Systems Agency, "Application Security Assessment Tool Market Survey," V3.0, July 29, 2004

NIST National Institute of Standards and Technology • Technology Administration • U.S. Department of Commerce

Web Service Tools*

- SOAPscope by Mindreef
- SOA Test by Parasoft

* Defense Information Systems Agency, "Application Security Assessment Tool Market Survey," V3.0, July 29, 2004

NIST National Institute of Standards and Technology • Technology Administration • U.S. Department of Commerce

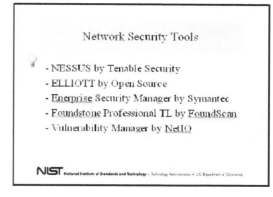

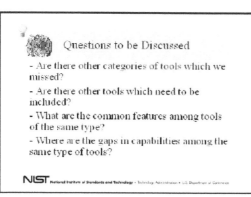

Elizabeth Fong: I want to do some scoping of the topic that we should be focusing on today . The subject is very broad and we want to do some preliminary warming up of defining tool categories. I want to start by looking at the tools that are out on the market. The tools being considered first for this workshopare software security tools.

Scope of tools to be included in the survey

Joe Jarzombek: Not all tools are listed by Liz' scope statement (requirements, modeling, server configuration flaws). Scope should include all SA tools, and not limit itself to tools that "just examine code".

Djenana Compara: You can't do security assurance without quality assurance. They are "intertwined".

Brian Chess: We need to start somewhere, however.

David Wichers: My question is on scope. Are you focusing toally on the software, or the operational environment that the software runs?

Elizabeth Fong: To narrow the scope, we should say that we are focusing on tools which have a security focus.

Paul Black: We will, in longer term, be going to look at all tools for software security assurance.

Ryan Berg: I completely agree that we need to limit the scope somehow.   We need to decide to set some boundaries.

Joe Jarzombek: But that's an inadequate boundary.

Sam Redwine: I don't mind if you say the scope is narrow.   This slide is all software security coding tools.

Attributes for categorization

Elizabeth Fong: It is difficult to classify some tools into certain categories, because these are like cherries and lemons.

John Peyton: We should differentiate between techniques and products (for instance code slicing is a technique, etc.). The language which the tool handles is an attribute, not a category.

Gary McGraw: We can ignore some of these tools, but the attackers won't ignore them.

Unattributed:

- Other attributes are cost, effort invested, how easy it is to install and use, and if it is only available as (used by) a service. Also some tools are open source versus commercial license.

- We should not categorize the tool by open source versus commercial license (the majority of the community).

- "Services" should be included in the survey, because services bring more value than a tool alone.

- What about "home grown tools"? Should that be in scope? How can you survey a tool that is not public?

William Pugh: Obviously we need to reduce scope of the survey to do anything worthwhile. Thre are too many classes of tools.

Paul Black: We have a larger program where we will be looking into other categories of tools.

What are outside of scope?

- The tool FXCop (*http://www.gotdotnet.com/team/fxcop/*) from Microsoft is a Binary Scanner. There are a lot more Dynamic Analyzers: Fuzzer, Purify.
- How about tools for real-time system?
- Network Scanners, firewalls, virus scanners, are all out of scope, and therefore should not be listed in the survey.

Elizabeth Fong: This categorization is based upon the Defense Information Systems Agency (DISA) report that is not publicly available. Instead of reinventing the wheel, we took the DISA report.

Tobie Jones: This report is not publicly available yet.

Taxonomy of Software Assurance Functions (Michael Kass)

NIST

Software Security Tool and Function Taxonomy

Michael Kass

National Institute of Standards and Technology

http://samate.nist.gov

michael.kass@nist.gov

Goals of this session

- Begin the definition of a software security tool taxonomy
- Prioritize tools in the taxonomy
  Based on (technology gaps, criticality, commonality..etc..)
- "Drill down" into an agreed-upon tool class and identify/prioritise key functions that define the tool

Why a Tool Taxonomy?

- Provide a common reference/classification of functions for evaluation of a tool's effectiveness
- A "first step" in defining a tool functional specification
- Tool specification becomes basis for creating tool reference dataset/benchmarks
- A common specification and reference dataset for comparing SA tools of the same class

Tool Taxonomy and Follow-on Products

71

A Taxonomy of Tools

Much of the information in the Software Security Tool Taxonomy is derived from the DISA Application Security Assessment Tool Survey, July 2004, to be published as a DISA STIG. Additionally, secure Software's CLASP Reference Guide V1.1 Training Manual was used to compile a list of common software vulnerability root causes.

- "External" Tools
  - Network Scanners
  - Web Application Scanners
  - Web Services Scanners
  - Dynamic Analysis Tools
- "Internal" Tools
  - Software Requirements Verification
  - Software Design/Model Verification
  - Source Code Scanners
  - Byte Code Scanners
  - Binary Code Scanners
  - Database Scanners

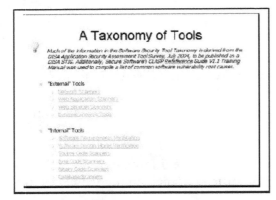
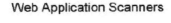

Network Scanners

Remotely scan targeted machines, performing port scans, and probing for vulnerabilities known in operating systems and third party network software.

- Functions – scan for known vulnerabilities in:
  - operating systems
  - applications
  - web servers
  - network devices
  - network protocols

Web Application Scanners

A more "specialized" class of SA tool that focuses specifically on web applications only, and are not considered generalized network scanners.

- Scan for known vulnerabilities by:
  - performing field manipulation
  - performing cooking poisoning

Web Services Scanner Functions

A relatively new class of SA tool whose purpose is the analysis of web service applications. Web service scanners have functions of the following type:

- Scan for known vulnerabilities by:
  - generate test cases from WSDL
  - support WS-I Test Tools
  - perform load testing
  - functional test of SOAP server
  - functional test of SOAP client
  - test XML encryption, signatures and signature verification
  - test WS-Security
  - perform XML validation of received messages

Dynamic Analysis Tool Functions

Dynamic analysis tools generate runtime vulnerability scenarios through the following functions:

- perform file corruption
- resource fault injection
- network fault injection
- system fault injection
- user interface fault injection
- design attacks
- implementation attacks

Software Requirements Verification Tool Functions

A suite of widely-used, peer-reviewed software requirements analysis tools does not exist today. However, functions of some tools that have been developed include determining whether requirements are: (from NASA's Automated Requirements Measurement Tool)

- complete
- consistent
- correct
- modifiable
- ranked
- traceable
- unambiguous
- understandable
- verifiable

Design/Model Verification Tool Functions

Design/model verification tools have the following functions:

- simulation
- exhaustive verification
- proof of design

Source Code Scanner Tool Functions

- identify vulnerabilities in code
- filter results (adjust false positives)
- generate a report of vulnerabilities (standard format?)
- categorize vulnerabilities (by severity, taxonomy?)
- scale to large code sets (should there be a code size/complexity benchmark?)
- generate code metrics (an accepted metric among same tools?)
- permit addition of new scanning rules
- perform trend analysis of code
- permit user annotation of code to inhibit flags at particular places

Identify Vulnerabilities

The ability to identify flaws that may lead to vulnerability varies from tool to tool, and the underlying techniques that they use. One of the first steps in comparing tools of the same class is to determine what software flaws all tools of that class should be able to identify. The following hierarchical classification of software flaw root causes is largely taken from Secure Software's CLASP V1.1 Training Manual

Range and Type Errors

5.2.1 Identify buffer overflow possibilities	5.2.15 Covert storage channel
5.2.2 Identify write-what-where vulnerabilities	5.2.16 Failure to account for default case in switch
5.2.3 Identify potential buffer underflow	5.2.18 Null pointer dereference
5.2.4 Identify integer overflow	5.2.19 Using freed memory
5.2.5 Find potential integer coercion situations	5.2.20 Double freeing memory
5.2.6 Unsized truncation error possibilities	5.2.21 Invoking untrusted mobile code
5.2.7 Sign extension error	5.2.22 Cross-site scripting
5.2.8 Integer coercion error	5.2.23 Format string problem
5.2.9 Unsize truncation error possibilities	5.2.24 Injection problem
5.2.10 Signed to unsigned conversion error	5.2.25 Command injection
5.2.11 Unsigned to signed conversion error	5.2.26 SQL injection
5.2.12 Unchecked array indexing	5.2.27 Deserialization of corrupted data
5.2.13 Miscalculated null termination	5.2.28 Identify divide-by-zero
5.2.14 Improper string length checking	5.2.29 Unvalidated input

Environmental Problems

5.3.1 Reliance on data layout
5.3.2 Relative path library search
5.3.3 Relying on package-level scope
5.3.4 Insufficient entropy in PRNG
5.3.5 Failure of TRNG
5.3.6 Publicizing of private data when using inner classes
5.3.7 Trust of system event data
5.3.8 Resource exhaustion (file descriptor, disk space, sockets, ...)
5.3.9 Information leak through class cloning
5.3.10 Information leak through serialization
5.3.11 Overflow of static internal buffer

Synchronization/Timing Errors

5.4.1 State synchronization error	5.4.13 Accidental leaking of sensitive information through error messages
5.4.2 Covert timing channel	
5.4.3 Symbolic name not mapping to correct object	5.4.14 Accidental leaking of sensitive information through sent data
5.4.4 Time of check, time of use race condition	5.4.15 Passing mutable objects to an untrusted method
5.4.5 Comparing classes by name	
5.4.6 Race condition in switch	5.4.16 Accidental leaking of sensitive information through data queries
5.4.7 Race condition in signal handler	
5.4.8 Unsafe function call from a signal handler	5.4.16 Race condition within a thread
5.4.9 Failure to drop privileges when reasonable	5.4.17 Reflection attack in an auth protocol
5.4.10 Race condition in checking for certificate revocation	5.4.18 Capture-replay
5.4.11 Mutable objects passed by reference	

Protocol Errors

5.5.1 Failure to follow chain of trust in certificate validation	5.5.13 Trusting self-reported DNS name
5.5.2 Key exchange without entity authentication	5.5.14 Using referrer field for authentication
5.5.3 Failure to validate host-specific certificate data	5.5.15 Using a broken or risky cryptographic algorithm
5.5.4 Failure to validate certificate expiration	5.5.16 Using password systems
5.5.5 Failure to check for certificate revocation	5.5.17 Using single-factor authentication
5.5.6 Failure to encrypt data	5.5.18 Not allowing password aging
5.5.7 Failure to add integrity check value	5.5.19 Allowing password aging
5.5.8 Failure to check integrity check value	5.5.20 Reusing a nonce, key pair in encryption
5.5.9 Use of hard-coded password	5.5.21 Using a key past its expiration date
5.5.10 Use of hard-coded cryptographic key	5.5.22 Not using a random IV with CBC mode
5.5.11 Storing passwords in a recoverable format	5.5.23 Failure to protect stored data from modification
5.5.12 Trusting self-reported IP address	5.5.24 Failure to provide confidentiality for stored data

Logic Errors

5.6.1 Ignored function return value	5.6.16 Improper cleanup on thrown exception
5.6.2 Missing parameter	5.6.17 Improper cleanup on thrown exception
5.6.3 Misinterpreted function return value	5.6.18 Uncaught exception
5.6.4 Uninitialized variable	5.6.19 Improper error handling
5.6.5 Duplicate key in associative list (alist)	5.6.20 Improper temp file opening
5.6.6 Deletion of data-structure sentinel	5.6.21 Guessed or visible temporary file
5.6.7 Addition of data-structure sentinel	5.6.22 Failure to deallocate data (memory leak)
5.6.8 Use of sizeof() on a pointer type	
5.6.9 Unintentional pointer scaling	5.6.23 Non-cryptographic PRNG
5.6.10 Improper pointer subtraction	5.6.24 Failure to check whether privileges were dropped successfully
5.6.11 Using the wrong operator	check for mismatched variable types
5.6.12 Assigning instead of comparing	identify unreachable code
5.6.13 Comparing instead of assigning	identify unnecessary code
5.6.14 Incorrect block delimitation	locate pointer errors (illegal dereferencing, uninitialized, null, functions)
5.6.15 Omitted break statement	

Byte Code Scanner Tool Functions

Static bytecode scanners are used in a similar fashion to source code scanners, and detect vulnerabilities through pattern recognition. This list of functions below is derived from the list of known security vulnerabilities identified by the FindBugs Java bytecode analyzer.

A method may expose internal representation by returning reference to mutable object
A method may expose internal representation by incorporating reference to mutable object
A finalizer should be protected, not public
A method may expose internal static state by storing a mutable object into a static field
A field isn't final and can't be protected from malicious code
A public static method may expose internal representation by returning array
A field should be both final and package protected
A field is a mutable array
A field is a mutable Hashtable
A field should be moved out of an interface and made package protected
A field should be package protected
A field isn't final but should be

Binary Code Scanner Tool Functions

Static binary code scanners are used in a similar fashion to source code scanners, however they detect vulnerabilities through disassembly and pattern recognition. One advantage that binary code scanners have over source code scanners is the ability to look at the compiled result, and factor in any vulnerabilities created by the compiler itself. Furthermore, library function code (not available to a source code scanner) can be examined as well. Some of the functions of these tools include:

- compare code against known malware signatures/patterns
- detect buffer overflows
- find missing format string
- identify wrong size specification
- identify incorrectly bounded buffer iteration

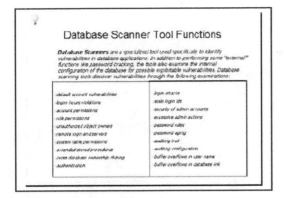

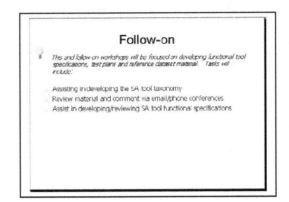

Michael Kass: Jeff Foster made a survey comparing three tools. Nick Rutar, Christian B. Almazan, and Jeffrey S. Foster - "A Comparison of Bug Finding Tools for Java" The 15th IEEE International Symposium on Software Reliability Engineering (ISSRE'04). Saint-Malo, Bretagne, France. November 2004.

Djenana Compara: We should not go by the technology limitation ("How to do it") of the tools. We should focus on "what" (What are the vulnerabilities).

William Pugh: This is scary because all tools do not do the same thing. Trying to create a chart for comparing tools would be difficult.

Unattributed: Classify/compare tools on their performance on a dataset, not by checking boxes <<of what they do or don't do>>.

Unattributed: The list of internal tools should also include compilers and editors.

David Jackson: We should drive <<software security>> from assurance requirements <<not from finding flaws>>

Stan Wisseman: Drive functional specifications from Common Criteria Protection Profiles.

Paul Black: Software Assurance Requirements driven tool analaysis is more in the domain of SA Common Body of Knowledge.

Unattributed: How do tools contribute to an assurance argument?

Joe Jarzombek: It would be great if EAL2 level of Common Criteria could be a "tool evaluation only"

Sam Redwine: <<We should take>> a prevention (proactive) vs. detection (reactive) stance. That is, concentrate on education, good design, etc. to write secure software in the first place, instead of concentrating on how to detect problems after the software is "done".

Unattributed:

- The majority think that a specification of what is buffer overflow is useful.
- Add code and design verification tools to Tool Functional Taxonomy (they are already in there)
- Code understanding tools or functions are important. <<For instance, debuggers, slicers, what functions calls this one, and what functions do I call.>>
- Slicing is more a technique than a tool.
- <<A tool that finds a flaw should>>
    - explain what the vulnerability is
    - give background and say is it exploitable
    - explain the reasoning, ie, why that is actually a vulnerability, eg, tainted data from function Q, still may have permissions through function Z, etc.
- The tool has to explain the vulnerability (undestand it). "How exploitable is it?"
- The last bullet (permit annotation of code) should be split into:
    - flags to interact with tool
    - annotation to improve the code

Recommended Best Practices, or, State of the Art in SA Tools (Brad Martin)

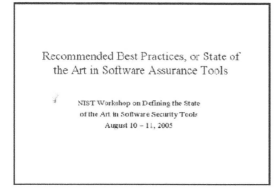

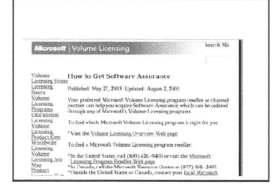
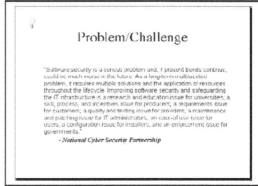

Software Security Education/Research?

The capacity as a nation to do the appropriate research and education to move the field of software security forward does not exist today.

- How can such a capacity be developed? A capacity for people with state-of-the-art knowledge, research support, and educational commitment necessary to create software systems to meet the national security requirements of the United States.
- Are adequate educational materials and capabilities available across the nation to educate new students and assist properly trained educators in teaching the most critical material in this area?

Software Security Education/Research?

- What software security certification accreditation programs currently exist? Should the Government, industry, and academia create a certification and accreditation program for increasing security in software development?
- Should secure software development accreditation guidelines be included as a mandatory component for designating NSA centers of excellence?
- Is a new academic discipline in secure software needed to provide our nation with graduates capable of producing secure software?

Process and Practices for Producing Secure Software?

No processes or practices have currently been shown to consistently produce secure software.

- **Process Models**
  - Are more effective practices that directly address security needed to handle these problems? (identification of threats, appropriate authentication, invalid authorization, appropriate partitioning, etc.)

Processes and Practices for Producing Secure Software?

- Do existing CMMs (CMMI, iCMM, SSE-CMM) adequately address software security?
- Are existing standards sufficient (ISO 9001:2000, EIA/IS 731, ISO/IEC 12207, ISO/IEC CD 15288)?

- **Secure Software Development Principles**
  - What is the effectiveness of threat modeling in reducing security vulnerabilities? Attack trees? Guidelines and checklists?
  - Is there sufficient empirical evidence of the benefits of using these techniques?

Process and Practices for Producing Secure Software?

Although numerous tools exist to support producing secure software (ranging from automated tools for verification and validation of formal specifications and design, to static code analyzers and checkers), no available tools and techniques can analyze large-scale software products and by themselves establish with high-confidence that no security problems exist in the specifications, design, or code.

- **Programming Languages**
  - What can be done to motivate the choice of programming languages where security vulnerabilities are inherently reduced?
  - Should academia be focused on designing new languages that include fundamental security features?

Process and Practices for Producing Secure Software?

- **Tools**
  - How are we to know which tools to use? There are so many choices:
    - Model checking – smv, cospan, sal
    - Software model checking – SPIN, Bandera, Java Pathfinder, Blast, MAGIC, Cadena, Verisoft
    - Theorem Provers – ACL2, HOL, Nuprl, PVS, Isabelle
    - Static and Dynamic Analysis – BANE, Cqual, Fluid, Polyspace, Prefix
  - Can programmers be asked to provide annotations to aid in the analysis of software?

Process and Practices for Producing Secure Software?

- **Tools**
  - Is synthesis of secure code from high-level specifications a more appropriate approach than analyzing/verifying low-level code?

  - How do we get the bugs that matter?
  - Is more analysis better?

Market for Lemons

"The market doesn't currently distinguish between cherries and lemons – it doesn't even encourage the development of cherries."
– Dave Wichers, Aspect Security

- Asymmetric information is carefully protected
  - Extremely difficult to analyze software (even with source)
  - Restrictive license agreements
  - Legal and regulatory restrictions on security analysts

- Virtually guarantees insecure software
  - If you can't tell the difference, why pay more?
  - No way to establish the benefit of secure software

- Only an idiot would develop and sell secure software
  - And if they try, they usually don't last long

References

- National Cyber Security Partnership,
- SSE-CMM,
- CMMI,
- iCMM,
- Open Web Application Security Project,
- Aspect Security,
  http://www.aspectsecurity.com/home.html

Brad Martin: My name is Brad Martin. I work for National Security Agency.

Education/Research

Sam Redwine: (Referring to Brad Martin's first slide on "Software Security Education/Research) We need to identify all additional knowledge one needs to produce good software.

Steve Christey: (Referring to Brad Martin's second slide on "Software Security Education/Research, last bullet: "Is a new academic discipline in secure software needed to provide our nation with graduates capable of producing secure software?) Security is not a new academic discipline. Our education process should roll-in security into academic discipline

Joe Jarzombak: Currently there are 60 – 80 centers of excellence through DHS, NSF. The software engineering common body of knowledge is another knowledge area. We still lack a computer science department that does not really view security as academically interesting, and the few computer science majors coming out do not meet the needs of the nation. However, we are getting some out of medical schools and business management department.

Don O'Neill: There is a difference between software *product* engineering and software *management* engineering. The object of the former is a good product. The object of the latter is cost, delivery date, etc.

Discussion about terms

Joe Jarzombak: We are trying to make sure that software assurance is embedded in the software. Some effort to get the definition out should be done by the community.

Djenana Campara: (Referring to term "Software defect" and "Software vulnerability) Software has weakness and symptoms.

Sam Redwine: We should distinguish between *probability* – chances of a breach, and *possibility* – is there a possible breach.

Processes and Practices for Producing Secure software

Gary McGraw: Quality is finding its way into software. This is because over the last few years, business extended out to produce more software. People come to understand how critical software is. Examples are Wall Street applications and cell phones.

James Nash: I've built safety related products, and it is still a probability that some code is unsafe. How can you say that software is safe?

Sam Redwine: There seems to be number of people that believe that having really good people will get you secure software. They've said a lot of airplanes fall out of the sky.

Michael Hicks: If you can solve the software problem, you can also solve the security problem.

Joe Jarzombek: (Referring to Brad Martin's second slide on "Processes and Practices for Producing Secure Software? First bullet: "Do existing CMMs adequately address software security?) The answer is no! The CMM's are not applicable to "small, shareware" software.

Choice of Programming Languages

Dave Wichers: (Referring to Brad Martin's third slide on "Process and Practices for Producing Secure Software? On Programming Languages). Let's talk about the benefits of adopting different languages to encourage people to move towards languages that are more secure.

Joe Jarzombek: By moving to different languages you are just moving to different sets of vulnerabilities. I would like a comparison that would compare this language to that language.

Steve Christey: The thesis behind what I am trying to say is any programming language that is out there now still has fundamental problems.

Joe Jarzombek: I agree. My point is for the languages that are out there, some quick summary that says what are the benefits of using one to the other. So for those who have the luxury of choosing a language, they can make a smarter choice. A lot of people don't have the luxury because they have legacy code.

Mark Fallon: Let's just rewrite all our network data and communication infrastructure in Java. Here are the business reasons of why people use the language. We are looking for developers to help build that product and when I try to bring in people it is all Java now.

Software Assurance Vulnerability List &Taxonomy (Mike Koo)

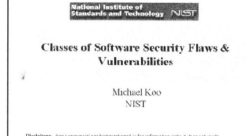

Classes of Software Security Flaws & Vulnerabilities

Michael Koo
NIST

Disclaimer: Any commercial product mentioned is for information only; it does not imply recommendation or endorsement by NIST nor does it imply that the products mentioned are necessarily the best available for the purpose.

NIST National Institute of Standards and Technology • Technology Administration • U.S. Department of Commerce

---

Definition of Software Security Flaws & Vulnerabilities

- *Software security flaws* - software defects, inadvertently or intentionally introduced, that violate the desired security properties of a computer or network system, such as confidentiality, integrity and availability.
- *Vulnerabilities* - flaws in a software product that can be exploited to compromise the security of computer or network system.

NIST National Institute of Standards and Technology • Technology Administration • U.S. Department of Commerce

---

Motivation for Classes of Software Security Flaws & Vulnerabilities

- *For Systematic Study* – classify security problems in software into categories that one can dissect for systematic study.
- *For SS Tools Evaluation* - a taxonomy of security vulnerability that the SA community would agree upon will be essential for evaluating Software Security (SS) tools and classifying SA functions.
- *For SRD Development* - Classes of software security flaws and vulnerabilities is one of resources to drive a standard reference dataset, which, in simply put, is a benchmark test suite for Software Security tools.

NIST National Institute of Standards and Technology • Technology Administration • U.S. Department of Commerce

---

Characteristics of Satisfactory Taxonomies [1]

- mutually exclusive - classifying in one category excludes all others because categories do not overlap,
- exhaustive - taken together, the categories include all possibilities,
- unambiguous - clear and precise so that classification is not uncertain, regardless of who is classifying,
- accepted - logical and intuitive so that they could become generally approved,
- Useful - can be used to gain insight into the field of inquiry.

[1] Edward G. Amoroso, *Fundamentals of Computer Security Technology*, Prentice-Hall PTR, Upper Saddle River, NJ, 1994.

NIST National Institute of Standards and Technology • Technology Administration • U.S. Department of Commerce

---

Examples of Computer & Network Security Taxonomies

- List of Vulnerabilities
  - Frederick B. Cohen, *Protection and Security on the Information Superhighway*, John Wiley & Sons, New York, 1995.
- List of Categories of Vulnerabilities
  - William R. Cheswick and Steven M. Bellovin, *Firewalls and Internet Security: Repelling the Wily Hacker*, Addison-Wesley Publishing Company, Reading, MA, 1994.
- List of Categories of Results
  - Deborah Russell and G. T. Gangemi, Sr., *Computer Security Basics*, O'Reilly & Associates, Inc., Sebastopol, CA, 1991.

NIST National Institute of Standards and Technology • Technology Administration • U.S. Department of Commerce

---

Examples of Computer & Network Security Taxonomies

- Matrices
  - T. Perry and P. Wallich, "Can Computer Crime Be Stopped?," *IEEE Spectrum*, Vol. 21, No. 5.

NIST National Institute of Standards and Technology • Technology Administration • U.S. Department of Commerce

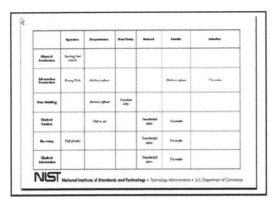

Examples of Computer & Network Security Taxonomies

- Tree Structure
  - Carl E. Landwehr, Alan R. Bull, John P. McDermott, and William S. Choi, "A Taxonomy of Computer Security Flaws," *ACM Computing Surveys*, Vol. 26, No. 3, September, 1994, pp. 211-254.

NIST National Institute of Standards and Technology • Technology Administration • U.S. Department of Commerce

---

Examples of Computer & Network Security Taxonomies

- Multiple Dimensions
  - John Howard, "An Analysis of Security Incidents on the Internet 1989-1995," PhD dissertation in Engineering and Public Policy, Carnegie Mellon University, 1997.

NIST National Institute of Standards and Technology • Technology Administration • U.S. Department of Commerce

---

Examples of Computer & Network Security Taxonomies

- Multiple Dimensions
  - Secure Software, Inc. "CLASP", 2005.
    - Three axes: Problem Type, Consequence, Exposure Period.

NIST National Institute of Standards and Technology • Technology Administration • U.S. Department of Commerce

---

Possible Goals of Classifying Software Security Flaws & Vulnerabilities

- A taxonomy that has classification categories with the satisfactory characteristics as possible.
- Incorporate commonly used terms in security vulnerabilities that occurred in modern days.
- Consensus from the SA community.

NIST National Institute of Standards and Technology • Technology Administration • U.S. Department of Commerce

---

Initial Draft

- Including vulnerabilities in server applications and client applications, e.g. UNIX programs (sendmail, BIND, etc), server-type program (ftp, http, irc, finger, etc.), mail clients (MS Outlook, Netscape mail, etc.), COTS, etc.
- Not including vulnerabilities related to network, computer system environment, configuration, system design, system access validation, etc.
- Each class of vulnerability may have a collection of subclasses. Each subclass is a variation of the class. The whole collection of subclass does not intend to fully represent that class.
- Each attack may exhibit any combination of the vulnerability classes and/or subclasses.

NIST National Institute of Standards and Technology • Technology Administration • U.S. Department of Commerce

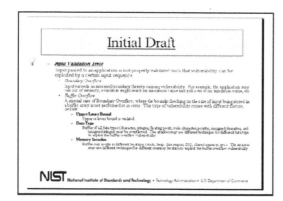

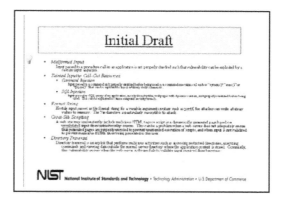

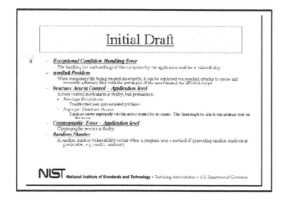

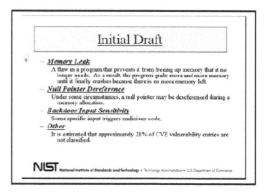

- Most vulnerabilities are composed with many factors => mutual exlusion will be difficult to deal with (examples : authentication problem, canonisation problem)
- Terminology (purportedly from Software Engineering Body of Knowledge (SWEBOK) We should be using this (McGraw)
  - o a flaw is a defect
  - o a vulnerability is a security problem
  - o a threat is a "bad actor", not a vulnerability
- Some of the proporties of the taxonomy will be difficult to achieve (i.e. some of the flaws cannot be identified by tools today)

- To have a taxonomy is important for the users and vendors.
- A taxonomy can serve as reference, resource "Common Body of Knowledge (CBK)".
- Need to be able to include backdoors.
- Design problems: RSA may be defect-free, but still vulnerable.
- Terminology: software weakness, software symptom should be used. (Djenana Campara)
- Program vulnerabilties are usually combinations of flaws.
- Taxonomy is to help us determine which tools or techniques could find or prevent certain flaws or classes of flaws.

- CVE's PLOVER taxonomy was introduced as a possible starting point
    - PLOVER structure – there will never be a "mutually exclusive" flaw taxonomy (e.g. is it an "authentication flaw" or a "logic flaw"?)
    - Does PLOVER fit the bill as a taxonomy? - PLOVER is a classification scheme and does not follow as a taxonomy.
    - What about CLASP? (CLASP uses different terminology, but PLOVER includes the same flaws)
    - Comment: 219 flaws is "too many"
    - CLASP/PLOVER may contain "unfindable" flaws… but is that any reason not to include them in a flaw taxonomy?

- Should classification be driven "top-down" (i.e. CC/PP requirements driven) or "bottom-up" (definition of flaws, then create test cases based upon those definitions)?

- Who has a taxonomy, Who wants to contribute to the taxonomy effort ?
    - Cigital/DHS (G. McGraw)
    - SEI/Cigital -> DISA <<same as above? Paul Black>>
    - PLOVER, Mitre (Steve Christey)
    - Ounce Lab
    - Klockwork
    - CLASP, Secure Software (J. Viega)
    - Fortify
    - OWASP - starting a project to rewrite "Top Ten." The granularity should not be overly small so that we have to handle over 200 flaw classes.

- For providing analysis of an application, both tool and service should be needed.
- It was suggested that a couple of examples (real vulnerability and false positive or "bad" and "fixed") be used in the reference dataset.

- => Action to do : The Samate Yahoo Group can host the different proposals of taxonomy.

- Terminology: threat vs. flaw vs. risk vs. ...
- Each <<entry>> should have code showing

- o (true) flaw
- o fixed code
- o false positive

the last two may be the same

- Suggestion: both "bugs" and "flaws" should be in the taxonomy.

Security metrics for Software and Tools (Paul Black)

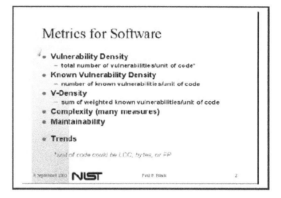
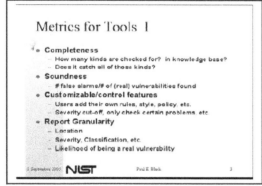
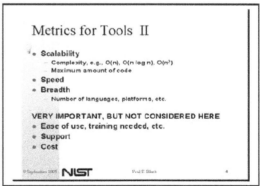

Sam Redwine: Who is the audience for the metrics?
Security Metrics for Software.

Paul E. Black: Metric must be multi-dimensional.

Djenana Campara: Don't "grade" code results: it threatens code developers in shops. Sometimes they would stubbornly argue that something was not a vulnerability, even though it was, just to get the grade up. So tool developers dropped "grades" from its software reports. It just lists flaws and vulnerabilities.

Joe Jarzombek: Confidence in tools should be high enough that Common Criteria EAL 2 should be a "tool-level application review".

Unattributed:

- Tool vendors are leery of "pass/fail reporting" on a potential government. contractor application results. They can be "sued" if that contractor loses a contract.
- Tools could measure for an applications's effective "countermeasures" (e.g. canaries to check for buffer overflow), or could use "resiliency" as a metric.
- Once you get to a certain point, you can't tell the difference between good code and great code. The metrics become too complex.
- There are no good "global metrics", that are, right for every need. Metrics can be local to a reviewing community's needs.
- An interesting study would be comparing actual security incidents with a metric as a way of providing validity to that metric.
- Granularity is hard to have with metrics. You might have "good" or "bad", but between is hard to define.
- Example of metrics : Number of "strcpy" call per 1000 lines of codes.

Metrics for Software Security Assessment Tools

First, one can ask, what (software) metrics does it generate?

David Melski: Look at medical lab tests for metric attributes, like specificity (precision), sensitivity (recall), accuracy, and positive predictive value.

Unattributed:

- Issue on the definition of soundness. Soundness is the number or possibility of false negatives. The notion of a "sound" tool or technique reverses if you're looking for flaws or freedom from flaws.
- Complexity may be a poor measure of scalability. The real item of interest is how fast it runs in practice. There was an algorithm that had 2^{2^n} run time, but ran very fast in practice. Maybe just give its speed for a number of cases, eg, small (1,000 LOC), medium (100K LOC), and big (1M LOC).
- Cost could be considered as attribute for a tool. Although reporting the cost in absolute dollars is tough because of different licensing agreements with different types of entities, changes in prices, etc., a simple quantizing might work: $ (cheap/free), $$ (moderate: hundreds of $), $$$ (expensive: thousands of dollars).
- Some tools provide aids to the user to fix the vulnerability (remediation)? Should that be a feature of all tools? Can it even be lumped in as a function with "flaw finding"?
- Should the tool explain the problem with descriptions, examples, flow traces, slices, etc.? Sometimes its hard to figure out why a tool thinks something is a flaw.
- Ease of use in terms of integration with IDE (Eclipse), make files, ANT
- Should workload (use of memory) be a tool metric?
- Soundness as a tool metric?

- Sensitivity as a too metric?
- Positive predictability as a tool metric?
- Completeness – what number of total flaws it detects

Reference Dataset (Mike Sindelar)

Designing a Reference Dataset

Michael Sindelar
NIST

Goals

- How should the reference dataset be constructed?
- What features are important?
- How should it be maintained and distributed?

Purpose

- A reference data set of code samples expressing security vulnerabilities could be used by consumers, developers, and researchers to identify strengths and weaknesses of Software Security tools
- The reference data set should be large scale effort and encompass as many vulnerabilities as possible

---

Construction

- Where should the code in the dataset come from?
- What sources would provide examples of many flaws, and real-life complexity?
- How large should code segments be?

Sources

- Academic Code
  - Code taken from course work
- Wild Type Code
  - Code taken from actual programs
- "Artificial Code"
  - Code written to express vulnerabilities

Construction

- What types of vulnerabilities are important to initially focus on?
- What are the tools currently focusing on?
- What languages are appropriate to start with?

Features

- What are important features that the reference data set should have?

- Should fixed and buggy code samples be linked together?

Features

- Information
  - Compiler, Language, Platform
- Code Source
  - Program Name, Academic, Wild Type, Artificial
- Flaws
  - Line Number, Entry in the Taxonomy, Bad Input
- Statistics
  - LOC, McCabe Complexity

Distribution

- What format for the reference dataset would be most useful? XML/SQL?

- How should updating the dataset be handled? Would a CVS repository be appropriate? Some other mechanism?

Maintenance

- Should the dataset be open or closed?

- How should additions to the reference dataset be handled? How would they be reviewed to ensure correctness?

- Who should maintain and distribute the dataset? Volunteers?

- Test Server or Testbed => people could run their dynamic scanner against it?
- If so, how would access to the testbed be controlled/accessed?
- Testing legacy software on "new" platforms is very difficult. Hence another argument for a testbed.
- Should a testbed be put behind firewall? Or limited to particular IP addresses?
- A testbed is a big maintenance issue. We need to be able to set up/wipe out/restore virtual environments easily.
- Need sample configuration environment (or a typical environment) to run Reference Data Set (RDS) (Karen Goertzel).
- What is the purpose of the testbed? For vendors? For users?
- We need version control on the code.
- Code (examples) should be added, never changed. The "meta-data" (flaws represented, xref to CVE, etc.) might change, but not the piece of code itself.
- There should be dynamic, as well as static, examples. That is, code to be examined by running it.
- Use of virtual machine could be a good idea (with possibility to reset it to its initial settings) (Sandbox, contained environment).

- Maybe there should be a "National Network Testbed" with known vulnerabilities that people could try their tools against. ("Network" because some vulnerabilities occur because of routers and other components)

  - We could configure a firewall to only allow access to certain IP addresses for certain. That way, you're never open to the whole world.
  - Run VMware (*http://www.vmware.com/*) images: they are easy to reload if one is crashed or corrupted.
  - Some tools would be installed (and run) within the testbed. Although they claim to run remotely, they do not.

- The product "SplashSuite" (used for shared memory applications) was mentioned.
- We should see what the antivirus community does in terms of testbeds.
- Others tools :
  - OWASP WebGoat
  - Foundstone (*http://www.foundstone.com/*) (The HacmeBook (*http://www.foundstone.com/index.htm?subnav=resources/navigation.htm&subcontent=/resources/proddesc/hacmebook.htm*) and the HacmeBank (*http://www.foundstone.com/index.htm?subnav=resources/navigation.htm&subcontent=/resources/proddesc/hacmebank.htm*)
  - Trade magazine test suites are another potential source of test material.

- The CVE can be a good start to build test (CVEs related to Open Source Project - code available).
- Issue : What do we do if new vulnerabilities are found in the test set ?
- Issue : Shall we annotate the test set code.

  - Adding annotations means changing the source code, therefore changing the lines of code.
  - We could have pairs (code with associated comment in 2 different files).
  - Using XML could give use a better documentation.
  - It's a bad idea to put annotations in the code (comment).
  - Code version number is essential.
  - Compiler version number would be a good thing.
  - Platform information as well.

- Wild code makes a "stronger case" for/against a tool than "manufactured code". (comment)
- Wild code will have to be a "community effort".
- Real-life examples should come from open source, widely used (so flaws are discovered), have a long history. Suggestion: sendmail.
- Can we get complexity in "manufactured code"?

- Some complex examples (requiring dataflow analysis) may have to be constructed "by hand".
- Will a CVS repository be enough? (not resolved).
- Issue : Test case coverage => completness. Do I cover all the type of buffer overflow?
- Complexity of certain type of code (industry code, etc.).
- How could we have a collaborative work on the test set ?

  - We could have a community front end (interface for contributors), where user decide if one piece of code is a vulnerability.
  - Editorial control should be given to trusted users only. We need moderators.
  - The code should go through a review process, then after examination it can be accepted as a full part of the dataset.
  - Have an "unverified" reference dataset next to a "verified" one.
  - Require a "common build script" that all submissions must use.
  - Who decide if a piece of code has a vulnerability ?
  - Rating of the code (star system, the more star it has the more confident we are that it's a vulnerability, like eBay or SlashDot karma).
  - Platform, compiler,... information about the code.
  - Consensus should be used to determine changes to reference dataset.
  - The security aspect should be considered (virus in dataset code) (Karen Goertzel).

- We should have a binary version of the data set for binary scanner and also for the purpose of running it on the corresponding platform (dynamic tools).
- We should keep the binaries, rather than depending on being able to recreate them from source, since compilers, etc. change.
- Need a strong sandbox/testbed for binary submissions.
- We need a "caveat emptor" (buyer beware) for any testbed code (source or binary).

Submission Process - How do people contribute RDS? Need some standard process or format.
- Maintenance of RDS can be a huge job.
- We can indicate RDS with levels: unverified/verified/reviewed/official.

Next Step(s) (Paul Black)

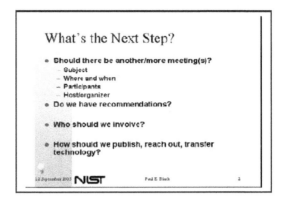

- There should be discussion groups for
  - taxonomy of flaws, about 8 people were interested in helping
  - reference dataset, about 10 people were interested in helping
  - software metrics
- We need to clearly identify who the users (customers) of the dataset, taxonomy, etc. are.

Elizaebth Fong: The workshop did not have anybody from the user community.

Paul E. Black: Bring in more "users" to the next workshop (Long Beach in November) including SCADA community, business, insurance, manufacturing, industry, etc.

Unattributed:

- We need to engage/invite people from the high assurance community, safety community, manufacturing community.
- Shall we involve other community? bad idea. It is better to scope our audience at this time, start small, since our project is so broad to begin with.

Karen Goertzel: On the other hand having users prevents us from going down the wrong path.

There was some discussion of the marketplace.

- Broadest: need (for more secure software)
  - state of the art (what is commercially available) is a subset of that
    - state of the practice is a subset of SoA

- Boomerang is the only reverse compiler tool

Develop Consensus on Workshop Report (Paul Black)

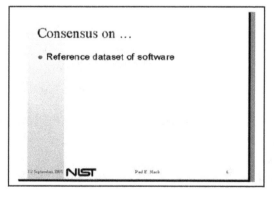

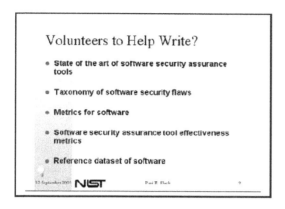

- The Semantic Web or Ontology tools might be used to align PLOVER, CLASP, etc. taxonomies. It would require annotation of HTML/XML to do this.

Unattributed:

- We should have fixed and broken version of code in the dataset. We should tell how to correct the vulnerability.
- How much assurance do I need? Or, given my risks, what assurance/tools do I need to give/use?
- Suggestion: If you can find 3 vendors who will support a Taxonomy of Flaws and and Reference Dataset, then go with it.

- State of the art in tools
    - sophistication of tools
    - technology assessment

- The code scanning tools vendors and users are still new at this.
    - Comparaison state of the art versus state of the practice.
    - Issue: the commercial tools are very proprietary (opaque). Vendors don't share with us what they can find.
    - Are companies "just" doing security assessments (or selling SSA tools) to motivate consumers to buy their real product, eg, firewall? consensus seemed to be, no.
    - Is the trend to "one stop shopping", eg, vendors that can assess your software, sell SSA tools, provide process stuff, and products (firewall, turn-key solutions)? Market is "converging" - multi-service companies are absorbing "point solution" companies (e.g Sanctum purchased Watchfire, Symantec purchased @stake). Still too early to tell.
- Are there more service companies than tool companies?
- Are the tools (or services) commercially viable?
    - Services are building the tools, then selling their service.
- Make the project more international: it's good to know what others are doing.
- Is lack of academic research due to funding or simply lack of interest?

- o Research – is not being done in academia.. It is a lot cheaper to make it a "consulting project" than to "advertise it" as research projects.
- o Academic community "forks off" a company, hence an "entrepreneurial function" takes over.
- o Dawson Engler's example is an exception to the rule. Most academic projects (tools) are small, generate papers, and disappear.
- o In the academic world, don't expect plugNplay tools. Expect long time period of development (5 years).
- o There IS a lot of research in academia. In contrast, research by companies is "behind closed doors"

- The taxonomy should have code samples or maybe associated exploits. Although exploits would be difficult to match with code. We should focus on the taxonomy (priority).
- Number of false positive is important to consider (overwhelming noise). False negative are important as well.
- Maturity of audience/user.
- A reference dataset MAY give us an idea how these companies fare against academic research projects.
- What is the start of the art of Software Assurance in overseas?

- o China, Russia, India? (SAMATE group needs to reach out beyond North America)

- Comment: Best chance of success is to "Keep It Simple". Start with taxonomy, work on descriptions of flaws, eventually create the exploit. (Begin with demonstrative examples, work toward compilable examples).

Metrics for tools:

- o False positives are the primary reason people don't use tools
- o Standardized reporting format would help (lots of noise in reports)
- o High/Medium/Low serverity is fairly meaningless.. what does it really mean?
- o False positives/useability issues are well understood
- o False negative (tool missing flaws) could be helped by a reference dataset

Action to do :

- o Send email asking who wants to participate to the workgroups. (Taxonomy, datasets, metrics)

Conclusions

This workshop generated many consensus, which are:

- The majority think that a shared reference dataset is a good idea. Through the SAMATE email list, volunteers will begin the process of defining the requirements and populating the SAMATE reference dataset, beginning with a small set of tests to demonstrate an "achievable" goal of testing and measuring the capabilities of SA tools.

- There were consensus that a common taxonomy of flaws is useful to users and vendors. Again, through the SAMATE email list, volunteers will begin to define the requirements of a software flaw and vulnerability taxonomy that all SA tool developers can agree upon and use as a reference for defining their tool's capabilities.

- All agreed that metrics for software and metrics for software assurance tool effectiveness will be a good idea, but did not reach consensus as to how to approach this challenge. This area will be discussed further in the SAMATE email list.

Submitted Material

Dynamic Buffer Overflow Detection[*]

Michael Zhivich
MIT Lincoln Laboratory
244 Wood Street
Lexington, MA 02420
mzhivich@ll.mit.edu

Tim Leek
MIT Lincoln Laboratory
244 Wood Street
Lexington, MA 02420
tleek@ll.mit.edu

Richard Lippmann
MIT Lincoln Laboratory
244 Wood Street
Lexington, MA 02420
lippmann@ll.mit.edu

ABSTRACT

The capabilities of seven dynamic buffer overflow detection tools (Chaperon, Valgrind, CCured, CRED, Insure++, ProPolice and TinyCC) are evaluated in this paper. These tools employ different approaches to runtime buffer overflow detection and range from commercial products to open-source gcc-enhancements. A comprehensive testsuite was developed consisting of specifically-designed test cases and model programs containing real-world vulnerabilities. Insure++, CCured and CRED provide the highest buffer overflow detection rates, but only CRED provides an open-source, extensible and scalable solution to detecting buffer overflows. Other tools did not detect off-by-one errors, did not scale to large programs, or performed poorly on complex programs.

Categories and Subject Descriptors

D.2.4 [**Software Engineering**]: Software/Program Verification; D.2.5 [**Software Engineering**]: Testing and Debugging; K.4.4 [**Computers and Society**]: Electronic Commerce Security

General Terms

Measurement, Performance, Security, Verification

---

*This work was sponsored by the Advanced Research and Development Activity under Air Force Contract F19628-00-C-0002. Opinions, interpretations, conclusions, and recommendations are those of the authors and are not necessarily endorsed by the United States Government.

2005 NIST Workshop on Defining the State of the Art in Software Security Tools, 2005 August 10-11, Gaithersburg, MD

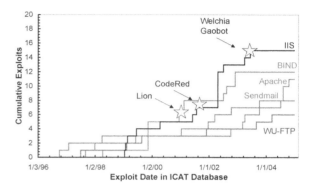

Figure 1: Cumulative exploits in commonly used server software.

Keywords

Security, buffer overflow, dynamic testing, evaluation, exploit, test, detection, source code

1. INTRODUCTION

Today's server software is under constant scrutiny and attack, whether for fun or for profit. Figure 1 shows the cumulative number of exploits found in commonly used server software, such as IIS, BIND, Apache, sendmail, and wu-ftpd. The stars indicate appearances of major worms, such as Lion, CodeRed and Welchia. As the data demonstrates, new vulnerabilities are still found, even in code that has been used and tested for years. A recent analysis by Rescorla [18] agrees with this observation, as it shows that vulnerabilities continue to be discovered at a constant rate in many types of software.

Buffer overflows enable a large fraction of exploits targeted at today's software. Such exploits range from arbitrary code execution on the victim's computer to denial of service (DoS) attacks. For 2004, CERT lists 3,780 vulnerabilities [3], while NIST reports that 75% of vulnerabilities in its ICAT database are remotely exploitable, of which 21% are due to buffer overflows [15]. Detecting and eliminating buffer overflows would thus make existing software far more secure.

There are several different approaches for finding and preventing buffer overflows. These include enforcing secure coding practices, statically analyzing source code, halting exploits via operating system support, and detecting buffer overflows at runtime [5]. Each approach has its advantages; however, each also suffers from limitations. Code reviews, no matter how thorough, will miss bugs. Static analysis seems like an attractive alternative, since the code is examined automatically and no test cases are required. However, current static analysis tools have unacceptably high false alarm rates and insufficient detection rates [24]. Operating system patches, such as marking stack memory non-executable, can only protect against a few types of exploits.

Dynamic buffer overflow detection and prevention is an attractive approach, because fundamentally there can be no false alarms. Tools that provide dynamic buffer overflow detection can be used for a variety of purposes, such as preventing buffer overflows at runtime, testing code for overflows, and finding the root cause of segfault behavior.

One disadvantage of using this approach to find errors in source code is that an input revealing the overflow is required, and the input space is generally very large. Therefore, dynamic buffer overflow detection makes the most sense as part of a system that can generate these revealing inputs. This evaluation is part of a project to create a grammar-based dynamic program testing system that enables buffer overflow detection in server software before deployment. Such a testing system will use the dynamic buffer overflow detection tool to find buffer overflows on a range of automatically-generated inputs. This will enable a developer to find and eliminate buffer overflows before the faults can be exploited on a production system. A similar testing approach is used in the PROTOS project at the University of Oulu [13].

This paper focuses on evaluating the effectiveness of current dynamic buffer overflow detection tools. A similar evaluation has been conducted by Wilander et al. [22], but it focused on a limited number of artificial exploits which only targeted buffers on the stack and in the bss section of the program. Our evaluation reviews a wider range of tools and approaches to dynamic buffer overflow detection and contains a more comprehensive test corpus.

The test corpus consists of two different testsuites. Section 3 presents the results for *variable-overflow* testsuite, which consists of 55 small test cases with variable amounts overflow, specifically designed to test each tool's ability to detect small and large overflows in different memory regions. Section 4 presents the results for 14 model programs containing remotely exploitable buffer overflows extracted from bind, wu-ftpd and sendmail.

The rest of the paper is organized as follows: Section 2 presents an overview of the tools tested in this evaluation, Sections 3 and 4 present descriptions and results for two different testsuites, Section 5 describes performance overhead incurred by the tools in this evaluation, and Section 6 summarizes and discusses our findings.

□ D□N□□IC □U□□□R O□□R□□O□ D□T□CTION TOO□□

This evaluation tests modern runtime buffer overflow detection tools including those that insert instrumentation at compile-time and others that wrap the binary executable directly. This section presents a short description of each tool, focusing on its strengths and weaknesses.

A summary of tool characteristics is presented in Table 1. A tool is considered to include *fine-grained bounds checking* if it can detect small (off-by-one) overflows. A tool *compiles large programs* if it can be used as a drop-in replacement for gcc and no changes to source code are needed to build the executable; however, minimal changes to the makefile are acceptable. The *time of error reporting* specifies whether the error report is generated when the error occurs or when the program terminates. Since program state is likely to become corrupted during an overflow, continuing execution after the first error may result in incorrect errors being reported. Instrumentation may also be corrupted, causing failures in error checking and reporting. If a tool can protect the program state by intercepting out-of-bounds writes before they happen and discarding them, reporting errors at termination may provide a more complete error summary.

□.1 □□é□□□□□ □ o□□□r□□□Too□s

Chaperon [16] is part of the commercial Insure toolset from Parasoft. Chaperon works directly with binary executables and thus can be used when source code is not available. It intercepts calls to malloc and free and checks heap accesses for validity. It also detects memory leaks and *read-before-write* errors. One limitation of Chaperon is that fine-grained bounds checking is provided only for heap buffers. Monitoring of buffers on the stack is very coarse. Some overflows are reported incorrectly because instrumentation can become corrupted by overflows. Like all products in the Insure toolset, it is closed-source which makes extensions difficult.

Valgrind [12] is an open-source alternative to Chaperon. It simulates code execution on a virtual x86 processor, and like Chaperon, intercepts calls to malloc and free that allow for fine-grained buffer overflow detection on the heap. After the program in simulation crashes, the error is reported and the simulator exits gracefully. Like Chaperon, Valgrind suffers from coarse stack monitoring. Also, testing is very slow (25 − 50 times slower than running the executable compiled with gcc [12]), since the execution is simulated on a virtual processor.

□.□ Co□□□□ër□□□sed Too□s

CCured [14] works by performing static analysis to determine the type of each pointer (SAFE, SEQ, or WILD). SAFE pointers can be dereferenced, but are not subject to pointer arithmetic or type casts. SEQ pointers can be used in pointer arithmetic, but cannot be cast to other pointer types, while WILD pointers can be used in a cast. Each pointer is instrumented to carry appropriate metadata at runtime - SEQ pointers include upper and lower bounds of the array they reference, and WILD pointers carry type tags. Appropriate checks are inserted into the executable based on pointer type. SAFE pointers are cheapest since they require only a NULL check, while WILD pointers are the most expensive, since they require type verification at runtime.

The main disadvantage of CCured is that the programmer may be required to annotate the code to help CCured determine pointer types in complex programs. Since CCured requires pointers to carry metadata, wrappers are needed to strip metadata from pointers when they pass to uninstrumented code and create metadata when pointers are received from uninstrumented code. While wrappers for commonly-used C library functions are provided with CCured, the de-

Tool	Version	OS	Requires Source	Open Source	Fine-grained Bounds Checking	Compiles Large Programs	Time of Error Reporting
Wait for segfault	N/A	Any	No	Yes	No	Yes	Termination
gcc	3.3.2	Linux	No	Yes	No	Yes	Termination
Chaperon	2.0	Linux	No	No	No*	Yes	Occurrence
Valgrind	2.0.0	Linux	No	Yes	No*	Yes	Termination
CCured	1.2.1	Linux	Yes	Yes	Yes	No	Occurrence
CRED	3.3.2	Linux	Yes	Yes	Yes	Yes	Occurrence
Insure++	6.1.3	Linux	Yes	No	Yes	Yes	Occurrence
ProPolice	2.9.5	Linux	Yes	Yes	No	Yes	Termination
TinyCC	0.9.20	Linux	Yes	Yes	Yes	No	Termination

Table 1: Summary of Tool Characteristics (* = fine-grained bounds checking on heap only)

veloper will have to create wrappers to interoperate with other uninstrumented code. These wrappers introduce another source of mistakes, as wrappers for sscanf and fscanf were incorrect in the version of CCured tested in this evaluation; however, they appear to be fixed in the currently-available version (v1.3.2).

C Range Error Detector (CRED) [19] has been developed by Ruwase and Lam, and builds on the Jones and Kelly "referent object" approach [11]. An *object tree*, containing the memory range occupied by all objects (i.e. arrays, structs and unions) in the program, is maintained during execution. When an object is created, it is added to the tree and when it is destroyed or goes out of scope, it is removed from the tree. All operations that involve pointers first locate the "referent object" – an object in the tree to which the pointer currently refers. A pointer operation is considered illegal if it results in a pointer or references memory outside said "referent object." CRED's major improvement is adhering to a more relaxed definition of the C standard – *out-of-bounds* pointers are allowed in pointer arithmetic. That is, an *out-of-bounds* pointer can be used in a comparison or to calculate and access an *in-bounds* address. This addition fixes false alarms that were generated in several programs compiled with Jones and Kelly's compiler, as pointers are frequently tested against an *out-of-bounds* pointer to determine a termination condition. CRED does not change the representation of pointers, and thus instrumented code can interoperate with unchecked code.

Two main limitations of CRED are unchecked accesses within library functions and treatment of structs and arrays as single memory blocks. The former issue is partially mitigated through wrappers of C library functions. The latter is a fundamental issue with the C standard, as casting from a struct pointer to a char pointer is allowed. When type information is readily available at compile time (i.e. the buffer enclosed in a struct is accessed via s.buffer[i] or s_ptr->buffer[i]), CRED detects overflows that overwrite other members within the struct. However, when the buffer inside a struct is accessed via an alias or through a type cast, the overflow remains undetected until the boundary of the structure is reached. These problems are common to all compiler-based tools, and are described further in Section 2.3.

Insure++ [16] is a commercial product from Parasoft and is closed-source, so we do not know about its internal workings. Insure++ examines source code and inserts instrumentation to check for memory corruption, memory leaks, memory allocation errors and pointer errors, among other things. The resulting code is executed, and errors are reported when they occur. Insure's major fault is its performance overhead, resulting in slowdown factor of up to 250 as compared to gcc. Like all tools, Insure's other limitation stems from the C standard, as it treats structs and arrays as single memory blocks. Since the product is closed-source, extensions are difficult.

ProPolice [8] is similar to StackGuard [6], and outperformed it on artificial exploits [22]. It works by inserting a "canary" value between the local variables and the stack frame whenever a function is called. It also inserts appropriate code to check that the "canary" is unaltered upon return from this function. The "canary" value is picked randomly at compile time, and extra care is taken to reorder local variables such that pointers are stored lower in memory than stack buffers.

The "canary" approach provides protection against the classic "stack smashing attack" [1]. It does not protect against overflows on the stack that consist of a single out-of-bounds write at some offset from the buffer, or against overflows on the heap. Since ProPolice only notices the error when the "canary" has changed, it does not detect read overflows or underflows. The version of ProPolice tested during this evaluation protected only functions that contained a character buffer, thus leaving overflows in buffers of other types undetected; this problem has been fixed in later versions by including -fstack-protector-all flag that forces a "canary" to be inserted for each function call.

Tiny C compiler (TinyCC) [2] is a small and fast C compiler developed by Fabrice Bellard. TinyCC works by inserting code to check buffer accesses at compile time; however, the representation of pointers is unchanged, so code compiled with TinyCC can interoperate with unchecked code compiled with gcc. Like CRED, TinyCC utilizes the "referent object" approach [11], but without CRED's improvements. While TinyCC provides fine-grained bounds checking of buffer accesses, it is much more limited than gcc in its capabilities. It failed to compile large programs such as Apache with the default makefile. It also does not detect read overflows, and terminates with a segfault whenever an overflow is encountered, without providing an error report.

2.3 Common Problems of Compiler-based Tools

There are two issues that appear in all of the compiler-based tools – unchecked accesses within library functions and treatment of structs and arrays as single memory blocks. The former problem is partially mitigated by creating wrappers for C library functions or completely reimplementing them. Creating these wrappers is error-prone, and many functions (such as File I/0) cannot be wrapped.

The latter problem is a fundamental issue with the C standard of addressing memory in arrays and structs. According to the C standard, a pointer to any object type can be cast to a pointer to any other object type. The result is defined by implementation, unless the original pointer is suitably aligned to use as a resultant pointer [17]. This allows the program to re-interpret the boundaries between struct members or array elements; thus, the only way to handle the situation correctly is to treat structs and arrays as single memory objects. Unfortunately, overflowing a buffer inside a struct can be exploited in a variety of attacks, as the same struct may contain a number of exploitable targets, such as a function pointer, a pointer to a `longjmp` buffer or a flag that controls some aspect of program flow.

□ □□RI□□□□□O□□R□□O□ T□□T□UIT□ □□□□U□TION

The *variable-overflow* testsuite evaluation is the first of two evaluations included in this paper. This testsuite is a collection of 55 small C programs that contain buffer overflows and underflows, adapted from Misha Zitser's evaluation of static analysis tools [24]. Each test case contains either a *discrete* or a *continuous* overflow. A *discrete* buffer overflow is defined as an out-of-bounds write that results from a single buffer access, which may affect up to 8 bytes of memory, depending on buffer type. A *continuous* buffer overflow is defined as an overflow resulting from multiple consecutive writes, one or more of which is out-of-bounds. Such an overflow may affect an arbitrary amount of memory (up to 4096 bytes in this testsuite), depending on buffer type and length of overflow.

Each test case in the variable-overflow testsuite contains a 200-element buffer. The overflow amount is controlled at runtime via a command-line parameter and ranges from 0 to 4096 bytes. Many characteristics of buffer overflows vary. Buffers differ in type (`char`, `int`, `float`, `func *`, `char *`) and location (stack, heap, data, bss). Some are in containers (struct, array, union, array of structs) and elements are accessed in a variety of ways (index, pointer, function, array, linear and non-linear expression). Some test cases include runtime dependencies caused by file I/O and reading from environment variables. Several common C library functions ((f)`gets`, (fs)`scanf`, `fread`, `fwrite`, `sprintf`, `str(n)cpy`, `str(n)cat`, and `memcpy`) are also used in test cases.

□.1 Tes□□ro□ed□re

Each test case was compiled with each tool, when required, and then executed with overflows ranging from 0 to 4096 bytes. A 0-byte overflow is used to verify a lack of false alarms, while the others test the tool's ability to detect small and large overflows. The size of a memory page on the Linux system used for testing is 4096 bytes, so an overflow of this size ensures a read or write off the stack page, which should segfault if not caught properly. Whenever the test required it, an appropriately sized file, input stream or environment variable was provided by the testing script. There are three possible outcomes of a test. A *detection* signifies

that the tool recognized the overflow and returned an error message. A *segfault* indicates an illegal read or write (or an overflow detection in TinyCC). Finally, a *miss* signifies that the program returned as if no overflow occurred.

Table 1 describes the versions of tools tested in our evaluation. All tests were performed on a Red Hat Linux release 9 (Shrike) system with dual 2.66GHz Xeon CPUs. The standard Red Hat Linux kernel was modified to ensure that the location of the stack with respect to *stacktop* address (0xC0000000) remained unchanged between executions. This modification was necessary to ensure consistent segfault behavior due to large overflows.

□.□ □□r□□□□□□□r□ow Tes□□□□□ Res□□□s

This section presents a summary of the results obtained with the variable-overflow testsuite. The graph in Figure 2 shows the fraction of test cases in the variable-overflow testsuite with a non-*miss* (*detection* or *segfault*) outcome for each amount of overflow (Higher fractions represents better performance. All test cases, with the exception of the 4 underflow test cases, are included on this graph even though the proportional composition of the testsuite is not representative of existing exploits. Nonetheless, the graph gives a good indication of tool performance. Fine-grained bounds checking tools are highlighted by the "fine-grained" box at the top of the graph.

The top performing tools are Insure++, CCured and CRED, which can detect small and large overflows in different memory locations. TinyCC also performs well on both heap and stack-based overflows, while ProPolice only detects continuous overflows and small discrete overflows on the stack. Since the proportion of stack-based overflows is larger than that of heap-based overflows in our testsuite, ProPolice is shown to have a relatively high fraction of detections. Chaperon and Valgrind follow the same shape as gcc, since these tools only provide fine-grained detection of overflows on the heap. This ability accounts for their separation from gcc on the graph.

As the graph demonstrates, only tools with fine-grained bounds checking, such as Insure++, CCured and CRED are able to detect small overflows, including off-by-one overflows, which can still be exploitable. For tools with coarse stack monitoring, a large increase in detections/segfaults occurs at the overflow of 21 bytes, which corresponds to overwriting the return instruction pointer. The drop after the next 4 bytes corresponds to the discrete overflow test cases, as they no longer cause a segfault behavior. ProPolice exhibits the same behavior for overflows of 9–12 bytes due to a slightly different stack layout. Tools with fine-grained bounds checking also perform better in detecting discrete overflows and thus do not exhibit these fluctuations. For very large overflows, all tools either detect the overflow or segfault, which results in fraction of non-*miss* outcomes close to 1, as shown on the far right side of the graph.

□ R□□□ □□□□□OIT □□□□□U□TION

Previously, we evaluated the ability of a variety of tools employing *static analysis* to detect buffer overflows [25]. These tools ranged from simple lexical analyzers to abstract interpreters [9, 10, 20, 21, 23]. We chose to test these tools against fourteen historic vulnerabilities in the popular Internet servers `bind`, `sendmail`, and `wu-ftpd`. Many of the detectors were unable to process the entire source for these

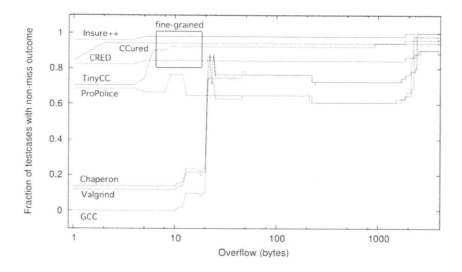

Figure 2: Combined fraction of detections and segfaults vs the amount of overflow in bytes. A box highlights tools with fine-grained bounds checking capabilities.

programs. We thus created *models* of a few hundred lines that reproduced most of the complexity present in the original. Further, for each model, we created a patched copy in which we verified that the overflow did not exist for a test input that triggered the error in the unpatched version. In that evaluation, we found that current static analysis tools either missed too many of these vulnerable buffer overflows or signaled too many false alarms to be useful. Here, we report results for seven dynamic overflow detectors on that same set of fourteen models of historic vulnerabilities. This provides a prediction of their performance on real overflows that occur in open-source servers.

.1 Tes⬚⬚ro⬚ed⬚re

During testing, each unpatched model program was compiled with the tool (if necessary) and executed on an input that is known to trigger the overflow. A *detection* signifies that the tool reported an overflow, while a *miss* indicates that the program executed as if no overflow occurred. A patched version of the model program was then executed on the same input. A *false alarm* was recorded if the instrumented program still reported a buffer overflow.

.⬚ Re⬚⬚⬚⬚⬚o⬚⬚Res⬚⬚s

Table 2 presents the results of this evaluation, which agree well with those on the variable-overflow testsuite. Three of the dynamic overflow detectors that provide fine-grained bounds checking, CCured, CRED, and TinyCC, work extremely well, detecting about 90% of the overflows whilst raising only one false alarm each. The commercial program Insure, which also checks bounds violations rigorously, fares somewhat worse with both fewer detections and more false alarms. Notice that misses and false alarms for these tools are errors in the implementation, and are in no way a fundamental limitation of dynamic approaches. For example, in the case of CRED the misses are due to an incorrect `memcpy` wrapper; there are no misses once this wrapper is

corrected. The CRED false alarm is the result of overly aggressive string length checks included in the wrappers for string manipulation functions such as `strchr`. None of the tools are given credit for a segmentation fault as a signal of buffer overflow (except TinyCC and gcc as this is the only signal provided). This is why, for instance, ProPolice appears to perform *worse* than gcc. As a final comment, it is worth considering the performance of gcc alone. If provided with the right input, the program itself detects almost half of these real overflows, indicating that input generation may be a fruitful area of future research.

⬚ ⬚⬚R⬚OR⬚ ⬚NC⬚ O⬚⬚R⬚⬚⬚D

The goals of the performance overhead evaluation are twofold. One is to quantify the slowdown caused by using dynamic buffer overflow detection tools instead of gcc when executing some commonly used programs. The other is to test each tool's ability to compile and monitor a complex program. In addition, this evaluation shows whether the tool can be used as a drop-in replacement for gcc, without requiring changes to the source code. Minimal modifications to the makefile are allowed, however, to accommodate the necessary options for the compilation process.

Our evaluation tests overhead on two common utility programs (`gzip` and `tar`), an encryption library (`OpenSSL`) and a webserver (`Apache`). For `OpenSSL` and `tar`, the testsuites included in the distribution were used. The test for `gzip` consisted of compressing a tar archive of the source code package for glibc (around 17MB in size). The test for `Apache` consisted of downloading a 6MB file 1,000 times on a loopback connection. The overhead was determined by timing the execution using `time` and comparing it to executing the test when the program is compiled with gcc. The results are summarized in Table 3. Programs compiled with gcc executed the tests in 7.2s (`gzip`), 5.0s (`tar`), 16.9s (`OpenSSL`) and 38.8s (`Apache`).

	Chaperon	Valgrind	CCured	CRED	gcc	Insure++	ProPolice	TinyCC
b1		d	d		d			d
b2		d	d		d			d
b3			d	d	d	d	d	d
b4	df	df	d	d	d	df	d	df
f1			d	d		d		d
f2			d	df		df		d
f3			d	d		d		d
s1			d	d		d		d
s2			d	d		df		d
s3			d	d				d
s4			d	d				d
s5			d	d		df	d	d
s6		df	d			d		
s7	d	d		d	d	d		d
$P(det)$	0.14	0.29	0.93	0.86	0.43	0.71	0.21	0.93
$P(fa)$	0.07	0.07	0.07	0.07	0	0.29	0	0.07

Table 2: Dynamic buffer overflow detection in 14 models of real vulnerabilities in open source server code. There are four `bind` models (b1–b4), three `wu-ftpd` models (f1–f3), and seven `sendmail` models (s1–s7). A 'd' indicates a tool detected a historic overflow, while an 'f' means the tool generated a false alarm on the patched version. $P(det)$ and $P(fa)$ are the fraction of model programs for which a tool signals a detection or false alarm, respectively.

Tool	gzip	tar	OpenSSL	Apache
Chaperon	75.6		61.8	
Valgrind	18.6	73.1	44.8	
CCured				
CRED	16.6	1.4	29.3	1.1
Insure++	250.4	4.7	116.6	
ProPolice	1.2	1.0	1.1	1.0
TinyCC				

Table 3: Instrumentation overhead for commonly used programs as a multiple of gcc execution time. The blank entries indicate that the program could not be compiled or executed with the corresponding tool.

Compiling and running `Apache` presented the most problems. Chaperon requires a separate license for multi-threaded programs, so we were unable to evaluate its overhead. Valgrind claims to support multi-threaded programs but failed to run due to a missing library. Insure++ failed on the configuration step of the makefile and thus was unable to compile `Apache`. CCured likewise failed at configuration, while TinyCC failed in parsing one of the source files during the compilation step.

The performance overhead results demonstrate some important limitations of dynamic buffer overflow detection tools. Insure++ is among the best performers on the variable-overflow testsuite; however, it incurs very high overhead. CCured and TinyCC, which performed well on both the variable-overflow testsuite and the model programs, cannot compile these programs without modifications to source code. CCured requires the programmer to annotate sections of the source code to resolve constraints involving what the tools considers "bad casts," while TinyCC includes a C parser that is likely incomplete or incorrect.

While CRED incurs large overhead on programs that involve many buffer manipulations, it has the smallest overhead for a fine-grained bounds checking tool. CRED can be used as a drop-in replacement for gcc, as it requires no changes to the source code in order to compile these programs. Only minimal changes to the makefile were required to enable bounds-checking and turn off optimizations. CRED's high detection rate, ease of use and relatively small overhead make it the best candidate for use in a comprehensive solution for dynamic buffer overflow detection.

⬜ DI⬜CU⬜⬜ION

The three top-performing tools in our evaluation are Insure++, CCured and CRED. Insure++ performs well on test cases, but not on model programs. It adds a large performance overhead, and the closed-source nature of the tool inhibits extensions. CCured shows a high detection rate and is open-source; however, it requires rewriting 1–2% of code to compile complicated programs [4]. CRED also offers a high detection rate, and it is open-source, easily extensible and has fairly low performance overhead (10% slowdown for simple Apache loopback test). Its main disadvantage is lack of overflow detection in library functions compiled without bounds-checking. Like all compiler-based tools, CRED does not detect overflows within structs in a general case; however, if the buffer enclosed in a struct is referenced directly, then CRED detects the overflow.

As this study demonstrates, several features are crucial to the success of a dynamic buffer overflow detection tool. Memory monitoring must be done on a fine-grained basis, as this is the only way to ensure that discrete writes and off-by-one overflows are caught. Buffer overflows in library functions, especially file I/O, often go undetected. Some tools solve this problem by creating wrappers for library functions, which is a difficult and tedious task. Recompiling libraries with the bounds-checking tool may be a better alternative, even if it should entail a significant slowdown. Error reporting is likewise essential in determining the cause of the problem because segfaults alone provide little information. Since instrumentation and messages can get corrupted by large overflows, the error should be reported immediately after the overflow occurs.

Of all the tools surveyed, CRED shows the most promise

as a part of a comprehensive dynamic testing solution. It offers fine-grained bounds checking, provides comprehensive error reports, compiles large programs and incurs reasonable performance overhead. It is also open-source and thus easily extensible. CRED is likewise useful for regression testing to find latent buffer overflows and for determining the cause of segfault behavior.

□ R□□□R□NC□□

[1] AlephOne. Smashing the stack for fun and profit. *Phrack Magazine*, 7(47), 1998.

[2] F. Bellard. TCC: Tiny C compiler. http://www.tinycc.org, Oct. 2003.

[3] CERT. CERT/CC statistics. http://www.cert.org/stats/cert_stats.html, Feb. 2005.

[4] J. Condit, M. Harren, S. McPeak, G. C. Necula, and W. Weimer. CCured in the real world. In *Proceedings of the ACM SIGPLAN 2003 conference on Programming language design and implementation*, pages 232–244. ACM Press, 2003.

[5] C. Cowan. Software security for open-source systems. *IEEE Security & Privacy*, 1(1):38–45, 2003.

[6] C. Cowan, C. Pu, D. Maier, J. Walpole, P. Bakke, S. Beattie, A. Grier, P. Wagle, Q. Zhang, and H. Hinton. Stackguard: Automatic adaptive detection and prevention of buffer-overflow attacks. In *Proceedings of the 7th USENIX Security Conference*, pages 63–78, San Antonio, Texas, Jan. 1998.

[7] N. Delgado, A. Q. Gates, and S. Roach. A taxonomy and catalog of runtime software-fault monitoring tools. *IEEE Transactions on Software Engineering*, 30(12):859–872, Dec. 2004.

[8] H. Etoh. GCC extension for protecting applications from stack smashing attacks. http://www.trl.ibm.com/projects/security/ssp/, Dec. 2003.

[9] D. Evans and D. Larochelle. Improving security using extensible lightweight static analysis. *IEEE Softw.*, 19(1):42–51, 2002.

[10] G. Holzmann. Static source code checking for user-defined properties. In *Proc. IDPT 2002*, Pasadena, CA, USA, June 2002.

[11] R. W. M. Jones and P. H. J. Kelly. Backwards-compatible bounds checking for arrays and pointers in C programs. In *Automated and Algorithmic Debugging*, pages 13–25, 1997.

[12] N. N. Julian Seward and J. Fitzhardinge. Valgrind: A GPL'd system for debugging and profiling x86-linux programs. http://valgrind.kde.org, 2004.

[13] R. Kaksonen. A functional method for assessing protocol implementation security. Publication 448, VTT Electronics, Telecommunication Systems, Kaitoväylä 1, PO Box 1100, FIN-90571, Oulu, Finland, Oct. 2001.

[14] G. C. Necula, S. McPeak, and W. Weimer. CCured: Type-safe retrofitting of legacy code. In *Proceedings of Symposium on Principles of Programming Languages*, pages 128–139, 2002.

[15] NIST. ICAT vulnerability statistics. http://icat.nist.gov/icat.cfm?function=statistics, Feb. 2005.

[16] Parasoft. Insure++: Automatic runtime error detection. http://www.parasoft.com, 2004.

[17] P. Plauger and J. Brodie. *Standard C*. PTR Prentice Hall, Englewood Cliffs, NJ, 1996.

[18] E. Rescorla. Is finding security holes a good idea? *IEEE Security & Privacy*, 3(1):14–19, 2005.

[19] O. Ruwase and M. Lam. A practical dynamic buffer overflow detector. In *Proceedings of Network and Distributed System Security Symposium*, pages 159–169, 2004.

[20] P. Technologies. PolySpace C verifier. http://www.polyspace.com/c.htm, Sept. 2001.

[21] D. Wagner, J. S. Foster, E. A. Brewer, and A. Aiken. A first step towards automated detection of buffer overrun vulnerabilities. In *Network and Distributed System Security Symposium*, pages 3–17, San Diego, CA, Feb. 2000.

[22] J. Wilander and M. Kamkar. A comparison of publicly available tools for dynamic buffer overflow prevention. In *Proceedings of the 10th Network and Distributed System Security Symposium*, pages 149–162, Feb. 2003.

[23] Y. Xie, A. Chou, and D. Engler. Archer: using symbolic, path-sensitive analysis to detect memory access errors. In *Proceedings of the 10th ACM SIGSOFT international symposium on Foundations of software engineering*, pages 327–336. ACM Press, 2003.

[24] M. Zitser. Securing software: An evaluation of static source code analyzers. Master's thesis, Massachusetts Institute of Technology, Department of Electrical Engineering and Computer Science, Aug. 2003.

[25] M. Zitser, R. Lippmann, and T. Leek. Testing static analysis tools using exploitable buffer overflows from open source code. *SIGSOFT Softw. Eng. Notes*, 29(6):97–106, 2004.

Using a Diagnostic Corpus of C Programs to Evaluate Buffer Overflow Detection by Static Analysis Tools*

Kendra Kratkiewicz
MIT Lincoln Laboratory
244 Wood Street
Lexington, MA 02420-9108
Phone: 781-981-2931
Email: KENDRA@LL.MIT.EDU

Richard Lippmann
MIT Lincoln Laboratory
244 Wood Street
Lexington, MA 02420-9108
Phone: 781-981-2711
Email: LIPPMANN@LL.MIT.EDU

ABSTRACT

A corpus of 291 small C-program test cases was developed to evaluate static and dynamic analysis tools designed to detect buffer overflows. The corpus was designed and labeled using a new, comprehensive buffer overflow taxonomy. It provides a benchmark to measure detection, false alarm, and confusion rates of tools, and also suggests areas for tool enhancement. Experiments with five tools demonstrate that some modern static analysis tools can accurately detect overflows in simple test cases but that others have serious limitations. For example, PolySpace demonstrated a superior detection rate, missing only one detection. Its performance could be enhanced if extremely long run times were reduced, and false alarms were eliminated for some C library functions. ARCHER performed well with no false alarms whatsoever. It could be enhanced by improving inter-procedural analysis and handling of C library functions. Splint detected significantly fewer overflows and exhibited the highest false alarm rate. Improvements in loop handling and reductions in false alarm rate would make it a much more useful tool. UNO had no false alarms, but missed overflows in roughly half of all test cases. It would need improvement in many areas to become a useful tool. BOON provided the worst performance. It did not detect overflows well in string functions, even though this was a design goal.

Categories and Subject Descriptors

D.2.4 [Software Engineering] Software/Program Verification, D.2.5 [Software Engineering] Testing and Debugging, K.4.4 [Computers and Society] Electronic Commerce Security.

General Terms

Measurement, Performance, Security, Verification.

Keywords

Security, buffer overflow, static analysis, evaluation, exploit, test, detection, false alarm, source code.

1. INTRODUCTION

Ideally, developers would discover and fix errors in programs before they are released. This, however, is an extremely difficult task. Among the many approaches to finding and fixing errors, static analysis is one of the most attractive. The goal of static

2005 NIST Workshop on Defining the State of the Art in Software Security Tools, 2005, August 10-11, Gaithersburg, MD.

analysis is to automatically process source code and analyze all code paths without requiring the large numbers of test cases used in dynamic testing. Over the past few years, static analysis tools have been developed to discover buffer overflows in C code.

Buffer overflows are of particular interest as they are potentially exploitable by malicious users, and have historically accounted for a significant percentage of the software vulnerabilities published each year [18, 20], such as in NIST's ICAT Metabase [9], CERT advisories [1], Bugtraq [17], and other security forums. Buffer overflows have also been the basis for many damaging exploits, such as the Sapphire/Slammer [13] and Blaster [15] worms.

A buffer overflow vulnerability occurs when data can be written outside the memory allocated for a buffer, either past the end or before the beginning. Buffer overflows may occur on the stack, on the heap, in the data segment, or the BSS segment (the memory area a program uses for uninitialized global data), and may overwrite from one to many bytes of memory outside the buffer. Even a one-byte overflow can be enough to allow an exploit [10]. Buffer overflows have been described at length in many papers, including [20], and many descriptions of exploiting buffer overflows can be found online.

This paper focuses on understanding the capabilities of static analysis tools designed to detect buffer overflows in C code. It extends a study by Zitser [20, 21] that evaluated the ability of several static analysis tools to detect fourteen known, historical vulnerabilities (all buffer overflows) in open-source software. The Zitser study first found that only one of the tools could analyze large, open-source C programs. To permit an evaluation, short, but often complex, model programs were extracted from the C programs and used instead of the original, much longer programs. Five static analysis tools were run on model programs with and without overflows: ARCHER [19], BOON [18], Splint [6, 12], UNO [8], and PolySpace C Verifier [14]. All use static analysis techniques, including symbolic analysis, abstract interpretation, model checking, integer range analysis, and inter-procedural analysis. Results were not encouraging. Only one of the five tools performed statistically better than random guessing. Not only did the tools fail to detect a significant number of overflows, but they also produced a large number of false alarms, indicating overflows where none actually existed. Equally discouraging were the confusion rates, reflecting the number of cases where a tool reports an error in both the vulnerable and patched versions of a program.

*This work was sponsored by the Advanced Research and Development Activity under Force Contract F19628-00-C-0002. Opinions, interpretations, conclusions, and recommendations are those of the authors and are not necessarily endorsed by the United States Government.

Given the small number of model programs, and the fact that buffer overflows were embedded in complex code, it is difficult to draw conclusions concerning why the tools performed poorly. This paper describes a follow-on analysis of the five tools evaluated in the previous study. It's simpler but broader, and more diagnostic test cases are designed to determine specific strengths and weaknesses of tools. Although this research evaluated only static analysis tools, it provides a taxonomy and test suite useful for evaluating dynamic analysis tools as well.

2. BUFFER OVERFLOW TAXONOMY

Using a comprehensive taxonomy makes it possible to develop test cases that cover a wide range of buffer overflows and make diagnostic tool assessments. Zitser developed a taxonomy containing thirteen attributes [20]. This taxonomy was modified and expanded to address problems encountered with its application, while still attempting to keep it small and simple enough for practical application. The new taxonomy consists of twenty-two attributes listed in Table 1.

Table 1. Buffer Overflow Taxonomy Attributes

Attribute Number	Attribute Name
1	Write/Read
2	Upper/Lower Bound
3	Data Type
4	Memory Location
5	Scope
6	Container
7	Pointer
8	Index Complexity
9	Address Complexity
10	Length/Limit Complexity
11	Alias of Buffer Address
12	Alias of Buffer Index
13	Local Control Flow
14	Secondary Control Flow
15	Loop Structure
16	Loop Complexity
17	Asynchrony
18	Taint
19	Runtime Environment Dependence
20	Magnitude
21	Continuous/Discrete
22	Signed/Unsigned Mismatch

Details on the possible values for each attribute are available in [11], and are summarized below. For each attribute, the possible values are listed in ascending order (i.e. the 0 value first).

Write/Read describes the type of memory access (write, read). While detecting illegal writes is probably of more interest in preventing buffer overflow exploits, it is possible that illegal reads could allow unauthorized access to information or could constitute one operation in a multi-step exploit.

Upper/Lower Bound describes which buffer bound is violated (upper, lower). While the term "buffer overflow" suggests an access beyond the upper bound of a buffer, it is equally possible to underflow a buffer, or access below its lower bound (e.g. buf[-1]).

Data Type indicates the type of data stored in the buffer (character, integer, floating point, wide character, pointer, unsigned character, unsigned integer). Character buffers are often manipulated with unsafe string functions in C, and some tools may focus on detecting overflows of those buffers; buffers of all types may be overflowed, however, and should be analyzed.

Memory Location indicates where the buffer resides (stack, heap, data region, BSS, shared memory). Non-static variables defined locally to a function are on the stack, while dynamically allocated buffers (e.g., those allocated by calling a malloc function) are on the heap. The data region holds initialized global or static variables, while the BSS region contains uninitialized global or static variables. Shared memory is typically allocated, mapped into and out of a program's address space, and released via operating system specific functions. While a typical buffer overflow exploit may strive to overwrite a function return value on the stack, buffers in other locations have been exploited and should be considered as well.

Scope describes the difference between where the buffer is allocated and where it is overrun (same, inter-procedural, global, inter-file/inter-procedural, inter-file/global). The scope is the same if the buffer is allocated and overrun within the same function. Inter-procedural scope describes a buffer that is allocated in one function and overrun in another function within the same file. Global scope indicates that the buffer is allocated as a global variable, and is overrun in a function within the same file. The scope is inter-file/inter-procedural if the buffer is allocated in a function in one file, and overrun in a function in another file. Inter-file/global scope describes a buffer that is allocated as a global in one file, and overrun in a function in another file. Any scope other than "same" may involve passing the buffer address as an argument to another function; in this case, the *Alias of Buffer Address* attribute must also be set accordingly. Note that the test suite used in this evaluation does not contain an example for "inter-file/global."

Container indicates whether the buffer resides in some type of container (no, array, struct, union, array of structs, array of unions). The ability of static analysis tools to detect overflows within containers (e.g., overrunning one array element into the next, or one structure field into the next) and beyond container boundaries (i.e., beyond the memory allocated for the container as a whole) may vary according to how the tools model these containers and their contents.

Pointer indicates whether the buffer access uses a pointer dereference (no, yes). Note that it is possible to use a pointer dereference with or without an array index (e.g. *pBuf or (*pBuf)[10]); the *Index Complexity* attribute must be set accordingly. In order to know if the memory location referred to by a dereferenced pointer is within buffer bounds, a code analysis tool must keep track of what pointers point to; this points-to analysis is a significant challenge.

Index Complexity indicates the complexity of the array index (constant, variable, linear expression, non-linear expression, function return value, array contents, N/A). This attribute applies only to the user program, and is not used to describe how buffer accesses are performed inside C library functions.

Address Complexity describes the complexity of the address or pointer computation (constant, variable, linear expression, non-linear expression, function return value, array contents). Again, this attribute is used to describe the user program only, and is not applied to C library function internals.

Length Complexity indicates the complexity of the length or limit passed to a C library function that overruns the buffer (N/A, none, constant, variable, linear expression, function return value, array contents). "N/A" is used when the test case does not call a C library function to overflow the buffer, whereas "none" applies when a C library function overflows the buffer, but the function does not take a length or limit parameter (e.g. strcpy). The remaining attribute values apply to the use of C library functions that do take a length or limit parameter (e.g. strncpy). Note that if a C library function overflows the buffer, the overflow is by definition inter-file/inter-procedural in scope, and involves at least one alias of the buffer address. In this case, the *Scope* and *Alias of Buffer Address* attributes must be set accordingly. Code analysis tools may need to provide their own wrappers for or models of C library functions in order to perform a complete analysis.

Alias of Buffer Address indicates if the buffer is accessed directly or through one or two levels of aliasing (no, one, two). Assigning the original buffer address to a second variable and subsequently using the second variable to access the buffer constitutes one level of aliasing, as does passing the original buffer address to a second function. Similarly, assigning the second variable to a third and accessing the buffer through the third variable would be classified as two levels of aliasing, as would passing the buffer address to a third function from the second. Keeping track of aliases and what pointers point to is a significant challenge for code analysis tools.

Alias of Buffer Index indicates whether or not the index is aliased (no, one, two, N/A). If the index is a constant or the results of a computation or function call, or if the index is a variable to which is directly assigned a constant value or the results of a computation or function call, then there is no aliasing of the index. If, however, the index is a variable to which the value of a second variable is assigned, then there is one level of aliasing. Adding a third variable assignment increases the level of aliasing to two. If no index is used in the buffer access, then this attribute is not applicable.

Local Control Flow describes what kind of program control flow most immediately surrounds or affects the overflow (none, if, switch, cond, goto/label, setjmp/longjmp, function pointer, recursion). For the values "if", "switch", and "cond", the buffer overflow is located within the conditional construct. "Goto/label" signifies that the overflow occurs at or after the target label of a goto statement. Similarly, "setjmp/longjmp" means that the overflow is at or after a longjmp address. Buffer overflows that occur within functions reached via function pointers are assigned the "function pointer" value, and those within recursive functions receive the value "recursion". The values "function pointer" and "recursion" necessarily imply a global or inter-procedural scope, and may involve an address alias. The *Scope* and *Alias of Buffer Address* attributes should be set accordingly.

Control flow involves either branching or jumping to another context within the program; hence, only path-sensitive code analysis can determine whether or not the overflow is actually reachable. A code analysis tool must be able to follow function pointers and have techniques for handling recursive functions in order to detect buffer overflows with the last two values for this attribute.

Secondary Control Flow has the same values as *Local Control Flow,* the difference being the location of the control flow construct. *Secondary Control Flow* either precedes the overflow or contains nested, local control flow. Some types of secondary control flow may occur without any local control flow, but some may not. The *Local Control Flow* attribute should be set accordingly.

The following example illustrates an if statement that precedes the overflow and affects whether or not it occurs. Because it precedes the overflow, as opposed to directly containing the overflow, it is labeled as secondary, not local, control flow.

```
int main(int argc, char *argv[])
{
   char buf[10];
   int i = 10;

   if (i > 10)
   {
      return 0;
   }

   /*  BAD  */
   buf[i] = 'A';

   return 0;
}
```

Only control flow that affects whether or not the overflow occurs is classified. In other words, if a preceding control flow construct has no bearing on whether or not the subsequent overflow occurs, it is not considered to be secondary control flow, and this attribute would be assigned the value "none."

The following example illustrates nested control flow. The inner if statement directly contains the overflow, and we assign the value "if" to the *Local Control Flow* attribute. The outer if statement represents secondary control flow, and we assign the value "if" to the *Secondary Control Flow* attribute as well.

```
int main(int argc, char *argv[])
{
   char buf[10];
   int i = 10;

   if (sizeof buf <= 10)
   {
      if (i <= 10)
      {
         /*  BAD  */
         buf[i] = 'A';
      }
   }

   return 0;
}
```

Some code analysis tools perform path-sensitive analyses, and some do not. Even those that do often must make simplifying approximations in order to keep the problem tractable and the solution scalable. This may mean throwing away some information, and thereby sacrificing precision, at points in the program where previous branches rejoin. Test cases containing secondary control flow may highlight the capabilities or limitations of these varying techniques.

☐oo☐☐☐r☐☐☐re☐ describes the type of loop construct within which the overflow occurs (none, standard for, standard do-while, standard while, non-standard for, non-standard do-while, non-standard while). A "standard" loop is one that has an initialization, a loop exit test, and an increment or decrement of a loop variable, all in typical format and locations. A "non-standard" loop deviates from the standard loop in one or more of these areas. Examples of standard `for`, `do-while`, and `while` loops are shown below, along with one non-standard `for` loop example:

Standard `for` loop:
```
for (i=0; i<11; i++)
{
    buf[i] = 'A';
}
```

Standard `do-while` loop:
```
i=0;
do
{
    buf[i] = 'A';
    i++;
} while (i<11);
```

Standard `while` loop:
```
i=0;
while (i<11)
{
    buf[i] = 'A';
    i++;
}
```

A non-standard `for` loop:
```
for (i=0; i<11; )
{
    buf[i++] = 'A';
}
```

Non-standard loops may necessitate secondary control flow (such as additional if statements). In these cases, the *Secondary Control Flow* attribute should be set accordingly. Any value other than "none" for this attribute requires that the *Loop Complexity* attribute be set to something other than "not applicable."

Loops may execute for a large number or even an infinite number of iterations, or may have exit criteria that depend on runtime conditions; therefore, it may be impossible or impractical for static analysis tools to simulate or analyze loops to completion. Different tools have different methods for handling loops; for example, some may attempt to simulate a loop for a fixed number of iterations, while others may employ heuristics to recognize and handle common loop constructs. The approach taken will likely affect a tool's capabilities to detect overflows that occur within various loop structures.

☐oo☐☐Co☐☐☐e☐☐y☐ indicates how many loop components (initialization, test, increment) are more complex than the standard baseline of initializing to a constant, testing against a constant, and incrementing or decrementing by one (N/A, none,

one, two, three). Of interest here is whether or not the tools handle loops with varying complexity in general, rather than which particular loop components are handled or not.

☐sy☐☐ro☐y☐ indicates if the buffer overflow is potentially obfuscated by an asynchronous program construct (no, threads, forked process, signal handler). The functions that may be used to realize these constructs are often operating system specific (e.g. on Linux, `pthread` functions; `fork`, `wait`, and `exit`; and `signal`). A code analysis tool may need detailed, embedded knowledge of these constructs and the O/S-specific functions in order to properly detect overflows that occur only under these special circumstances.

T☐☐☐ describes whether a buffer overflow may be influenced externally (no, argc/argv, environment variables, file read or stdin, socket, process environment). The occurrence of a buffer overflow may depend on command line or stdin input from a user, the value of environment variables (e.g. `getenv`), file contents (e.g. `fgets`, `fread`, or `read`), data received through a socket or service (e.g. `recv`), or properties of the process environment, such as the current working directory (e.g. `getcwd`). All of these can be influenced by users external to the program, and are therefore considered "taintable." These may be the most crucial overflows to detect, as it is ultimately the ability of the external user to influence program operation that makes exploits possible. As with asynchronous constructs, code analysis tools may require detailed modeling of O/S-specific functions in order to properly detect related overflows. Note that the test suite used in this evaluation does not contain an example for "socket."

R☐☐☐e☐☐☐ro☐☐e☐☐De☐e☐de☐☐e☐ indicates whether or not the occurrence of the overrun depends on something determined at runtime (no, yes). If the overrun is certain to occur on every execution of the program, it is not dependent on the runtime environment; otherwise, it is.

☐ ☐☐☐☐de☐ indicates the size of the overflow (none, 1 byte, 8 bytes, 4096 bytes). "None" is used to classify the "OK" or patched versions of programs that contain overflows. One would expect static analysis tools to detect buffer overflows without regard to the size of the overflow, unless they contain an off-by-one error in their modeling of library functions. The same is not true of dynamic analysis tools that use runtime instrumentation to detect memory violations; different methods may be sensitive to different sizes of overflows, which may or may not breach page boundaries, etc. The various overflow sizes were chosen with future dynamic tool evaluations in mind. Overflows of one byte test both the accuracy of static analysis modeling, and the sensitivity of dynamic instrumentation. Eight and 4096 byte overflows are aimed more exclusively at dynamic tool testing, and are designed to cross word-aligned and page boundaries.

Co☐☐☐o☐s☐D☐s☐re☐e☐ indicates whether the buffer overflow jumps directly out of the buffer (discrete) or accesses consecutive elements within the buffer before overflowing past the bounds (continuous). Loop constructs are likely candidates for containing continuous overflows. C library functions that overflow a buffer while copying memory or string contents into it demonstrate continuous overflows. An overflow labeled as continuous should have the loop-related attributes or the Length Complexity attribute (indicating the complexity of the length or limit passed to a C library function) set accordingly. Some dynamic tools rely on "canaries" at buffer boundaries to detect continuous overflows [5], and therefore may miss discrete overflows.

█████ed █ █s ███ed ██ █S█ ██████indicates if the buffer overflow is caused by using a signed or unsigned value where the opposite is expected (no, yes). Typically, a signed value is used where an unsigned value is expected, and gets interpreted as a very large unsigned or positive value, causing an enormous buffer overflow.

This taxonomy is specifically designed for developing simple diagnostic test cases. It may not fully characterize complex buffer overflows that occur in real code, and specifically omits complex details related to the overflow context.

For each attribute (except for Magnitude), the zero value is assigned to the simplest or "baseline" buffer overflow, shown below:

```
int main(int argc, char *argv[])
{
  char buf[10];
  /*  BAD  */
  buf[10] = 'A';
  return 0;
}
```

Each test case includes a comment line as shown with the word "BAD" or "OK." This comment is placed on the line before the line where an overflow might occur and it indicates whether an overflow does occur. The buffer access in the baseline program is a write operation beyond the upper bound of a stack-based character buffer that is defined and overflowed within the same function. The buffer does not lie within another container, is addressed directly, and is indexed with a constant. No C library function is used to access the buffer, the overflow is not within any conditional or complicated control flows or asynchronous program constructs, and does not depend on the runtime environment. The overflow writes to a discrete location one byte beyond the buffer boundary, and cannot be manipulated by an external user. Finally, it does not involve a signed vs. unsigned type mismatch.

Appending the value digits for each of the twenty-two attributes forms a string that classifies a buffer overflow, which can be referred to during results analysis. For example, the sample program shown above is classified as "0000000000000000000100." The single "1" in this string represents a "Magnitude" attribute indicating a one-byte overflow. This classification information appears in comments at the top of each test case file, as shown in the example below:

```
/* Taxonomy Classification: 0000000000000000000000 */
```

```
/*
 * WRITE/READ          0       write
 * WHICH BOUND         0       upper
 * DATA TYPE           0       char
 * MEMORY LOCATION     0       stack
 * SCOPE               0       same
 * CONTAINER           0       no
 * POINTER             0       no
 * INDEX COMPLEXITY    0       constant
 * ADDRESS COMPLEXITY  0       constant
 * LENGTH COMPLEXITY   0       N/A
```

```
 * ADDRESS ALIAS              0       none
 * INDEX ALIAS                0       none
 * LOCAL CONTROL FLOW         0       none
 * SECONDARY CONTROL FLOW     0       none
 * LOOP STRUCTURE             0       no
 * LOOP COMPLEXITY            0       N/A
 * ASYNCHRONY                 0       no
 * TAINT                      0       no
 * RUNTIME ENV. DEPENDENCE    0       no
 * MAGNITUDE                  0       no overflow
 * CONTINUOUS/DISCRETE        0       discrete
 * SIGNEDNESS                 0       no
 */
```

While the Zitser test cases were program pairs consisting of a bad program and a corresponding patched program, this evaluation uses program quadruplets. The four versions of each test case correspond to the four possible values of the Magnitude attribute; one of these represents the patched program (no overflow), while the remaining three indicate buffer overflows of one, eight, and 4096 bytes denoted as minimum, medium, and large overflows.

█ T██T █UIT█

A full discussion of design considerations in creating test cases is provided in [11]. Goals included avoiding tool bias; providing samples that cover the taxonomy; measuring detections, false alarms, and confusions; naming and documenting test cases to facilitate automated scoring and encourage reuse; and maintaining consistency in programming style and use of programming idioms.

Ideally, the test suite would have at least one instance of each possible buffer overflow that could be described by the taxonomy. Unfortunately, this is completely impractical. Instead, a "basic" set of test cases was built by first choosing a simple, baseline example of a buffer overflow, and then varying its characteristics one at a time. This strategy results in taxonomy coverage that is heavily weighted toward the baseline attribute values. Variations were added by automated code-generation software that produces C code for the test cases to help insure consistency and make it easier to add test cases.

Four versions of 291 different test cases were generated with no overflow and with minimum, medium, and large overflows. Each test case was compiled with gcc, the GNU C compiler [7], on Linux to verify that the programs compiled without warnings or errors (with the exception of one test case that produces an unavoidable warning). Overflows were verified using CRED, a fine-grained bounds-checking extension to gcc that detects overflows at run time [16], or by verifying that the large overflow caused a segfault. A few problems with test cases that involved complex loop conditions were also corrected based on initial results produced by the PolySpace tool.

█ T██T █ROC█DUR███

The evaluation consisted of analyzing each test case (291 quadruplets), one at a time using the five static analysis tools (ARCHER, BOON, PolySpace, Splint, and UNO), and collecting tool outputs. Tool-specific Perl programs parsed the output and determined whether a buffer overflow was detected on the line immediately following the comment in each test case. Details of the test procedures are provided in [11]. No annotations were added and no modifications were made to the source code for any tool.

Since BOON does not report line numbers for the errors, automated tabulation cannot validate that the reported error corresponds to the commented buffer access in the test case file. Instead, it assumes that any reported error is a valid detection. Therefore, BOON detections and false alarms were further inspected manually to verify their accuracy, and some were dismissed (two detections and two false alarms) since they did not refer to the buffer access in question.

Special handling was required for PolySpace in cases where the buffer overflow occurs in a C library function. PolySpace reports the error in the library function itself, rather than on the line in the test case file where the function is called. Therefore, the results tabulator looks for errors reported in the called library function and counts those detections irrespective of the associated line number. Additionally, one test case involving wide characters required additional command-line options to work around errors reported when processing wctype h.

5 RESULTS AND ANALYSIS

All five static analysis tools performed the same regardless of overflow size (this would not necessarily hold for dynamic analysis). To simplify the discussion, results for the three magnitudes of overflows are thus reported as results for "bad" test cases as a whole.

Table 2 shows the performance metrics computed for each tool. The detection rate indicates how well a tool detects the known buffer overflows in the bad programs, while the false alarm rate indicates how often a tool reports a buffer overflow in the patched programs. The confusion rate indicates how well a tool can distinguish between the bad and patched programs. When a tool reports a detection in both the patched and bad versions of a test case, the tool has demonstrated "confusion." The formulas used to compute these three metrics are shown below:

$$\text{detection rate} = \frac{\text{\# test cases where tool reports overflow in bad version}}{\text{\# test cases tool evaluated}}$$

$$\text{false alarm rate} = \frac{\text{\# test cases where tool reports overflow in patched version}}{\text{\# of test cases tool evaluated}}$$

$$\text{confusion rate} = \frac{\text{\# test cases where tool reports overflow in both bad and patched version}}{\text{\# test cases where tool reports overflow in bad version}}$$

As seen in Table 2, ARCHER and PolySpace both have detection rates exceeding 90%. PolySpace's detection rate is nearly perfect, missing only one out of the 291 possible detections. PolySpace produced seven false alarms, whereas ARCHER produced none. Splint and UNO each detected roughly half of the overflows. Splint, however, produced a substantial number of false alarms, while UNO produced none. Splint also exhibited a

fairly high confusion rate. In over twenty percent of the cases where it properly detected an overflow, it also reported an error in the patched program. PolySpace's confusion rate was substantially lower, while the other three tools had no confusions. BOON's detection rate across the test suite was extremely low.

Table 2. Overall Error Report Statistics Tested in Test Cases

Tool	Detection Rate	False Error Rate	Confusion Rate
ARCHER	90.7%	0.0%	0.0%
BOON	0.7%	0.0%	0.0%
PolySpace	99.7%	2.4%	2.4%
Splint	56.4%	12.0%	21.3%
UNO	51.9%	0.0%	0.0%

It is important to note that it was not necessarily the design goal of each tool to detect every possible buffer overflow. BOON, for example, focuses only on the misuse of string manipulation functions, and therefore is not expected to detect other overflows. It is also important to realize that these performance rates are not necessarily predictive of how the tools would perform on buffer overflows in actual, released code. The basic test suite used in this evaluation was designed for diagnostic purposes, and the taxonomy coverage exhibited is not representative of that which would be seen in real-world buffer overflows.

Figure 1 presents a plot of detection rate vs. false alarm rate for each tool. Each tool's performance is plotted with a single data point representing detection and false alarm percentages. The diagonal line represents the hypothetical performance of a random guesser that decides with equal probability if each commented buffer access in the test programs results in an overflow or not. The difference between a tool's detection rate and the random guesser's is only statistically significant if it lies more than two standard deviations (roughly 6 percentage points when the detection rate is 50%) away from the random guesser line at the same false alarm rate. In this evaluation, every tool except BOON performs significantly better than a random guesser. In Zitser's evaluation [20], only PolySpace was significantly better. This difference in performance reflects the simplicity of the diagnostic test cases.

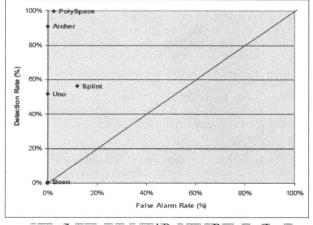

Figure 1. False Alarm and Detection Rates per Tool

Since PolySpace missed only one detection, and three of the other tools did detect the overflow in that test case, one could obtain perfect detection across the evaluation test suite by using PolySpace as the primary authority, and using one of the other tool's results only when PolySpace did not detect an overflow. ARCHER or UNO would be the best choice for this, as neither adds false alarms.

Similarly combining ARCHER and Splint would produce a detection rate of ninety-eight percent. ARCHER missed twenty-seven detections, and Splint detected all but five of those. Unfortunately, using Splint would also add thirty-five false alarms.

T□□e□. Too□□□e□□□□□T□es□

Too□	To□□□T□□e□□Se□s□□	□□er□□e T□□e□□er□Tes□□ C□se□Se□s□□
ARCHER	288	0.247
BOON	73	0.063
PolySpace	200,820 (56 hrs)	172.526
Splint	24	0.021
UNO	27	0.023

Execution times for the five tools were measured as the total time to run each test case, including tool startup time, and are provided in Table 3. PolySpace's high detection rate comes at the cost of dramatically long execution times. ARCHER demonstrated both the second highest detection rate and the second highest execution time. Splint and UNO, with intermediate detection rates, had the two fastest execution times. BOON's slightly longer execution time did not result in a higher detection rate.

Some general observations can be made from inspecting the results as a whole. Missed detections and false alarms tend to group in certain attribute sets and follow logical patterns. If one tool missed a detection on a particular test case, usually some of the other tools missed it as well. For five test cases, only PolySpace did not miss detections in the bad programs. No attribute sets and no individual test cases have perfect detections across all five tools, but eight attribute sets contain no false alarms at all (Upper/Lower Bound, Data Type, Pointer, Alias of Buffer Index, Loop Structure, Loop Complexity, Asynchrony, and Signed/Unsigned Mismatch). Without the BOON results, looking exclusively at the results of the other four tools, three of the attribute sets (Write/Read, Data Type, and Alias of Buffer Index) and 108 individual test cases had perfect detections across the four tools. Complete and detailed results are presented in [11].

□. De□□□ed Too□ D□□□□os□□s□

The following paragraphs discuss each tool's performance in detail, especially compared to the tools' design goals.

□RC□□R□s strategy is to detect as many bugs as possible while minimizing the number of false alarms. It is designed to be inter-procedural, path-sensitive, context-sensitive, and aware of pointer aliases. It performs a fully-symbolic, bottom-up data flow analysis, while maintaining symbolic constraints between variables (handled by a linear constraint solver). ARCHER checks array accesses, pointer dereferences, and function calls that take a pointer and size. It is hard-coded to recognize and handle a small number of memory-related functions, such as malloc [19].

The authors discuss many limitations of the current version of ARCHER. It does not handle function pointers, and imposes a five second limit on the analysis of any particular function. Furthermore, it loses precision after function calls, as it does not perform a proper inter-procedural side effects analysis and has a very simple alias analysis. It does not understand C library string functions, nor does it keep track of null pointers or the length of null-terminated strings. Its linear constraint solver is limited to handling at most two non-linearly related variables. Finally, some of the techniques it uses to reduce false alarms will necessarily result in missed detections. For instance, if no bounds information is known about a variable used as an array index, ARCHER assumes the array access is trusted and does not issue a warning. Similarly, it only performs a bounds check on the length and offset of a pointer dereference if bounds information is available; otherwise it remains quiet and issues no warning [19].

With close to a 91% detection rate and no false alarms, ARCHER performs well. Most of its twenty-seven missed detections are easily explained by its limitations. Twenty of these were inter-procedural, and this seems to be ARCHER's main weakness. The twenty inter-procedural misses include fourteen cases that call C library functions. While the authors admit to ignoring string functions, one might have expected memcpy() to be one of the few hard-coded for special handling. The other inter-procedural misses include cases involving shared memory, function pointers, recursion, and simple cases of passing a buffer address through one or two functions. Of the remaining seven misses, three involve function return values, two depend on array contents, and two involve function pointers and recursion.

While some of the missed detections occurred on cases whose features may not be widespread in real code (such as recursion), the use of C library functions and other inter-procedural mechanisms are surely prevalent. Indeed, ARCHER's poor performance in [20] is directly attributable to the preponderance of these features. ARCHER detected only one overflow in this prior evaluation, which was based on overflows in real code. Of the thirteen programs for which ARCHER reported no overflows, twelve contained buffer overflows that would be classified according to this evaluation's taxonomy as having inter-procedural scope, and nine of those involve calls to C library functions. To perform well against a body of real code, ARCHER needs to handle C library functions and other inter-procedural buffer overflows correctly.

□OON□s analysis is flow-insensitive and context-insensitive for scalability and simplicity. It focuses exclusively on the misuse of string manipulation functions, and the authors intentionally sacrificed precision for scalability. BOON will not detect overflows caused by using primitive pointer operations, and ignores pointer dereferencing, pointer aliasing, arrays of pointers, function pointers, and unions. The authors expect a high false alarm rate due to the loss of precision resulting from the compromises made for scalability [18].

In this evaluation, BOON properly detected only two out of fourteen string function overflows, with no false alarms. The two detected overflows involve the use of strcpy() and fgets(). BOON failed to detect the second case that calls strcpy(), all six cases that call strncpy(), the case that calls getcwd, and all four cases that call memcpy(). Despite the heavy use of C library string functions in [20], BOON achieved only two detections in that evaluation as well.

□o□y□□□è is the only commercial tool included in this evaluation. Details of its methods and implementation are proprietary. We do know, however, that its approach uses techniques described in several published works, including: symbolic analysis, or abstract interpretation [2]; escape analysis, for determining inter-procedural side effects [4]; and inter-procedural alias analysis for pointers [3]. It can detect dead or unreachable code. Like other tools, it may lose precision at junctions in code where previously branched paths rejoin, a compromise necessary to keep the analysis tractable.

PolySpace missed only one detection in this evaluation, which was a case involving a signal handler. The PolySpace output for this test case labeled the signal handler function with the code "UNP," meaning "unreachable procedure." PolySpace reported seven false alarms across the test suite. These included all four of the taint cases, shared memory, using array contents for the buffer address, and one of the calls to strcpy(). The false alarm on the array contents case is not too surprising, as it is impractical for a tool to track the contents of every location in memory. PolySpace does not, however, report a false alarm on the other two cases involving array contents. The other six false alarms are on test cases that in some way involve calls to C library or O/S-specific function calls. Not all such cases produced false alarms, however. For instance, only one out of the two strcpy() cases produced a false alarm: the one that copies directly from a constant string (e.g., "AAAA"). Without more insight into the PolySpace implementation, it is difficult to explain why these particular cases produced false alarms.

PolySpace did not perform as well in Zitser's evaluation [20]. Again, without more knowledge of the tool's internals, it is difficult to know why its detection rate was lower. Presumably the additional complexity of real code led to approximations to keep the problem tractable, but at the expense of precision. The majority of the false alarms it reported in Zitser's evaluation were on overflows similar to those for which it reported false alarms in this evaluation: those involving memory contents and C library functions.

PolySpace's performance comes with additional cost in money and in time. The four other tools were open source when this evaluation was performed, and completed their analyses across the entire corpus in seconds or minutes. PolySpace is a commercial program and ran for nearly two days and eight hours, averaging close to three minutes of analysis time per test case file. This long execution time may make it difficult to incorporate into a code development cycle.

□□□□□employs "lightweight" static analysis and heuristics that are practical, but neither sound nor complete. Like many other tools, it trades off precision for scalability. It implements limited flow-sensitive control flow, merging possible paths at branch points. Splint uses heuristics to recognize loop idioms and determine loop bounds without resorting to more costly and accurate abstract evaluation. An annotated C library is provided, but the tool relies on the user to properly annotate all other

functions to support inter-procedural analysis. Splint exhibited high false alarm rates in the developers' own tests [6, 12].

The basis test suite used in this evaluation was not annotated for Splint for two reasons. First, it is a more fair comparison of the tools to run them all against the same source code, with no special accommodations for any particular tool. Second, expecting developers to completely and correctly annotate their programs for Splint seems unrealistic.

Not surprisingly, Splint exhibited the highest false alarm rate of any tool. Many of the thirty-five false alarms are attributable to inter-procedural cases; cases involving increased complexity of the index, address, or length; and more complex containers and flow control constructs. The vast majority, 120 out of 127, of missed detections are attributable to loops. Detections were missed in all of the non-standard for() loop cases (both discrete and continuous), as well as in most of the other continuous loop cases. The only continuous loop cases handled correctly are the standard for loops, and it also produces false alarms on nearly all of those. In addition, it misses the lower bound case, the "cond" case of local flow control, the taint case that calls getcwd, and all four of the signed/unsigned mismatch cases.

While Splint's detection rate was similar in this evaluation and the Zitser evaluation [20], its false alarm rate was much higher in the latter. Again, this is presumably because code that is more complex results in more situations where precision is sacrificed in the interest of scalability, with the loss of precision leading to increased false alarms.

Splint's weakest area is loop handling. Enhancing loop heuristics to more accurately recognize and handle non-standard for loops, as well as continuous loops of all varieties, would significantly improve performance. The high confusion rate may be a source of frustration to developers, and may act as a deterrent to Splint's use. Improvements in this area are also important.

UNO is an acronym for uninitialized variables, null-pointer dereferencing, and out-of-bounds array indexing, which are the three types of problems it is designed to address. UNO implements a two-pass analysis; the first pass performs intra-procedural analysis within each function, while the second pass performs a global analysis across the entire program. It appears that the second pass focuses only on global pointer dereferencing, in order to detect null pointer usage; therefore, UNO would not seem to be inter-procedural with respect to out-of-bounds array indexing. UNO determines path infeasibility, and uses this information to suppress warnings and take shortcuts in its searches. It handles constants and scalars, but not computed indices (expressions on variables, or function calls), and easily loses precision on conservatively-computed value ranges. It does not handle function pointers, nor does it attempt to compute possible function return values. Lastly, UNO does not handle the setjmp/longjmp construct [8].

UNO produced no false alarms in the basic test suite, but did miss nearly half of the possible detections (140 out of 291), most of which would be expected based on the tool's description. This included every inter-procedural case, every container case, nearly every index complexity case (the only one it detected was the simple variable), every address and length complexity case, every address alias case, the function and recursion cases, every signed/unsigned mismatch, nearly every continuous loop, and a small assortment of others. It performed well on the various data types, index aliasing, and discrete loops. Given the broad variety of detections missed in the basic test suite, it is not surprising that UNO exhibited the poorest performance in Zitser's evaluation [20].

⬜ CONC⬜U⬜ION⬜

A corpus of 291 small C-program test cases was developed to evaluate static and dynamic analysis tools that detect buffer overflows. The corpus was designed and labeled using a new, comprehensive buffer overflow taxonomy. It provides a benchmark to measure detection, false alarm, and confusion rates of tools, and can be used to find areas for tool enhancement. Evaluations of five tools validate the utility of this corpus and provide diagnostic results that demonstrate the strengths and weaknesses of these tools. Some tools provide very good detection rates (e.g. ARCHER and PolySpace) while others fall short of their specified design goals, even for simple uncomplicated source code. Diagnostic results provide specific suggestions to improve tool performance (e.g. for Splint, improve modeling of complex loop structures; for ARCHER, improve inter-procedural analysis). They also demonstrate that the false alarm and confusion rates of some tools (e.g. Splint) need to be reduced.

The test cases we have developed can serve as a type of litmus test for tools. Good performance on test cases that fall within the design goals of a tool is a prerequisite for good performance on actual, complex code. Additional code complexity in actual code often exposes weaknesses of the tools that result in inaccuracies, but rarely improves tool performance. This is evident when comparing test case results obtained in this study to results obtained by Zitser [20] with more complex model programs. Detection rates in these two studies are shown in Table 4. As can be seen, the two systems that provided the best detection rates on the model programs (PolySpace and Splint) also had high detection rates on test cases. The other three tools performed poorly on model programs and either poorly (BOON) or well (ARCHER and UNO) on test cases. Good performance on test cases (at least on the test cases within the tool design goals) is a necessary but not sufficient condition for good performance on actual code. Finally, poor performance on our test corpus does not indicate that a tool doesn't provide some assistance when searching for buffer overflows. Even a tool with a low detection rate will eventually detect some errors when used to analyze many thousands of lines of code.

T⬜⬜⬜.Co⬜⬜rso⬜o⬜de⬜⬜⬜o⬜r⬜⬜s w⬜⬜⬜⬜l ⬜⬜s⬜⬜ses⬜⬜d ⬜ w⬜⬜⬜ ⬜⬜ore ⬜⬜o⬜ ⬜⬜⬜ode⬜⬜ro⬜r⬜⬜s⬜⬜⬜⬜⬜ser⬜⬜⬜⬜

Too⬜	Tes⬜C⬜se De⬜⬜⬜ö⬜	⬜ode⬜ ⬜ro⬜r⬜⬜ De⬜⬜⬜ö⬜⬜⬜⬜⬜⬜
ARCHER	90.7%	1%
BOON	0.7%	5%
PolySpace	99.7%	87%
Splint	56.4%	57%
UNO	51.9%	0.0%

The test corpus could be improved by adding test cases to cover attribute values currently underrepresented, such as string functions. It may also be used to evaluate the performance of dynamic analysis approaches. Anyone wishing to use the test corpus should send email to the authors.

⬜ ⬜CKNO⬜ ⬜⬜D⬜⬜ ⬜NT⬜

We would like to thank Rob Cunningham and Tim Leek for discussions, and Tim for help with getting tools installed and running. We also thank David Evans for his help with Splint, David Wagner for answering questions about BOON, Yichen Xie and Dawson Engler for their help with ARCHER, and Chris Hote and Vince Hopson for answering questions about C-Verifier and providing a temporary license.

⬜ R⬜⬜⬜R⬜NC⬜⬜

[1] CERT (2004). CERT Coordination Center Advisories, http://www.cert.org/advisories/, Carnegie Mellon University, Software Engineering Institute, Pittsburgh, PA

[2] Cousot, P. and Cousot, R. (1976). Static determination of dynamic properties of programs, *Proceedings of the 2nd International Symposium on Programming,* Paris, France, 106--130

[3] Deutsch, A. (1994). Interprocedural may-alias analysis for pointers: beyond *k*-limiting, *Proceedings of the ACM SIGPLAN'94 Conference on Programming Language Design and Implementation*, Orlando, Florida, 230--241

[4] Deutsch, A. (1997). On the complexity of escape analysis, *Proceedings of the 24th ACM SIGPLAN-SIGACT Symposium on Principles of Programming Languages,* Paris, France, 358--371

[5] Etoh, H. (2004). GCC extension for protecting applications from stack smashing attacks, http://www.trl.ibm.com/projects/security/ssp/

[6] Evans, D. and Larochelle, D. (2002). Improving security using extensible lightweight static analysis, *IEEE Software,* 19 (1), 42--51

[7] GCC Home Page (2004). Free Software Foundation, Boston, MA, http://gcc.gnu.org/

[8] Holzmann, G. (2002). UNO: Static source code checking for user-defined properties, Bell Labs Technical Report, Bell Laboratories, Murray Hill, NJ, 27 pages

[9] ICAT (2004). The ICAT Metabase, http://icat.nist.gov/icat.cfm, National Institute of Standards and Technology, Computer Security Division, Gaithersburg, MD

[10] klog (1999). The frame pointer overwrite, *Phrack Magazine,* 9 (55), http://www.tegatai.com/~jbl/overflow-papers/P55-08

[11] Kratkiewicz, K. (2005). Evaluating Static Analysis Tools for Detecting Buffer Overflows in C Code, Master's Thesis, Harvard University, Cambridge, MA, 285 pages

[12] Larochelle, D. and Evans, D. (2001). Statically detecting likely buffer overflow vulnerabilities, *Proceedings of the 10th USENIX Security Symposium*, Washington, DC, 177--190

[13] Moore, D., Paxson, V., Savage, S., Shannon, C., Staniford, S., and Weaver, N. (2003). The Spread of the Sapphire/Slammer Worm, http://www.caida.org/outreach/papers/2003/sapphire/sapphire.html

[14] PolySpace Technologies (2003). PolySpace C Developer Edition, http://www.polyspace.com/datasheets/c_psde.htm, Paris, France

[15] PSS Security Response Team (2003). PSS Security Response Team Alert - New Worm: W32.Blaster.worm, http://www.microsoft.com/technet/treeview/default.asp?url=/technet/security/alerts/msblaster.asp, Microsoft Corporation, Redmond, WA

[16] Ruwase, O. and Lam, M. (2004). A practical dynamic buffer overflow detector, *Proceedings of the 11th Annual Network and Distributed System Security Symposium*, San Diego, CA, 159--169

[17] Security Focus (2004). The Bugtraq mailing list, http://www.securityfocus.com/archive/1, SecurityFocus, Semantec Corporation, Cupertino, CA

[18] Wagner, D., Foster, J.S., Brewer, E.A., and Aiken, A. (2000). A first step towards automated detection of buffer overrun vulnerabilities, *Proceedings of the Network and Distributed System Security Symposium*, San Diego, CA, 3--17

[19] Xie, Y., Chou, A., and Engler, D. (2003). ARCHER: Using symbolic, path-sensitive analysis to detect memory access errors, *Proceedings of the 9th European Software Engineering Conference/10th ACM SIGSOFT International Symposium on Foundations of Software Engineering*, Helsinki, Finland, 327--336

[20] Zitser, M. (2003). Securing Software: An Evaluation of Static Source Code Analyzers, Master's Thesis, Massachusetts Institute of Technology, Cambridge, MA, 130 pages

[21] Zitser, M., Lippmann, R., and Leek, T. (2004). Testing static analysis tools using exploitable buffer overflows from open-source code, *Proceedings of the 12th ACM SIGSOFT International Symposium on Foundations of Software Engineering*, Newport Beach, CA, 97--106

Static Analysis of Binary Executable Code

Thomas W. Reps[1,2], Tim Teitelbaum[1,3], Paul Anderson[1], and David Melski[1]

[1] GrammaTech, Inc.
[2] University of Wisconsin
[3] Cornell University

The Context. A substantial percentage of all US coding jobs will be outsourced to China, Israel, Russia, the E.U., and India in the coming decade. On top of the trend toward outsourcing, there is increasing deployment of COTS software—for which source code is often unavailable—in presumably secure national and DoD information systems. Moreover, legacy code—for which design documents are usually out-of-date, and for which source code is sometimes unavailable and sometimes non-existent—will continue to be left deployed.

The Problem. What is needed are ways to determine whether third-party and legacy application programs can perform malicious operations (or can be induced to perform malicious operations), and to be able to make such judgments in the absence of source code.

Our Vision. We aim to advance the state of the art in software assurance—in particular, to address the problem of finding bugs and security vulnerabilities in programs when source code is unavailable. Our goal is to create a platform, CodeSurfer/x86 [2, 3] that carries out static analysis on executables and provides information that an analyst can use to understand the workings of potentially malicious code, such as COTS components, plugins, mobile code, and DLLs. A second goal is to use this platform to create tools [4] that an analyst can employ to determine such information as

- whether a program contains inadvertent security vulnerabilities

- whether a program contains deliberate security vulnerabilities, such as back doors, time bombs, or logic bombs. If so, the goal is to provide information about activation mechanisms, payloads, and latencies.

Recent research in programming languages, software engineering, and computer security has led to new kinds of tools for analyzing code for bugs and security vulnerabilities [4-7, 9-14]. In these tools, static analysis is used to determine a conservative answer to the question "Can the program reach a bad state?" In principle, such tools would be of great help to an analyst trying to detect malicious code hidden in software, except for one important detail: the aforementioned tools all focus on analyzing source code written in a high-level language; as will be discussed shortly, there are a number of reasons why analyses that start from source code do not provide the right level of detail for checking certain kinds of properties, which can cause bugs, security vulnerabilities, and malicious behavior to be invisible to such tools.

In contrast, there are many advantages to analyzing executables:

- An executable contains the actual instructions that will be executed, and hence provides information that reveals the actual behavior that arises during program execution. This information includes

- memory-layout details, such as (i) the positions (i.e., offsets) of variables in the run-time stack's activation records, and (ii) padding between fields of a struct.

- register usage

- execution order (e.g., of actual parameters)

- optimizations performed

- artifacts of compiler bugs

Access to such information can be crucial; for instance, many security exploits depend on platform-specific features, such as the structure of activation records. Vulnerabilities can escape notice when a tool does not have information about adjacency relationships among variables. In contrast, such information is hidden from tools that work on intermediate representations (IRs) that are built directly from the source code.

- By analyzing executables, the entire program can be analyzed---including libraries that are linked to the program. Because library code can be analyzed directly, it is not necessary to rely on the potentially unsound models of library functions that are typically used when analyzing source code.

- An executable may have been modified subsequent to compilation, e.g., to insert malicious code. Such modifications are not visible to tools that analyze source code.

- Source-code-analysis tools are only applicable when source code is available, which limits their usefulness in security applications (e.g., to analyzing code from open-source projects).

- The source code may have been written in more than one language. This complicates the life of designers of tools that analyze source code because multiple languages must be supported, each with their own quirks. A tool that analyzes executables only needs to support one language.

- Even if the source code is primarily written in one high-level language, it may contain inlined assembly code in selected places. Source-level tools typically either skip over inlined assembly code [8] or do not push the analysis beyond sites of inlined assembly code [1].

We have embarked on the creation of a new generation of software-analysis and software-assurance tools based on analyzing executables. Such tools can reap the aforementioned benefits of analyzing executables to provide a level of precision that would not otherwise be possible.

References

[1] PREfast with driver-specific rules, October 2004. http://www.microsoft.com/whdc/devtools/tools/PREfast-drv.mspx.

[2] G. Balakrishnan and T. Reps. Analyzing memory accesses in x86 executables. In Comp. Construct., pages 5–23, 2004.

[3] Balakrishnan, G., Gruian, R., Reps, T., and Teitelbaum, T., CodeSurfer/x86 – A platform for analyzing x86 executables, (tool demonstration paper). To appear in Proc. Int. Conf. on Compiler Construction, April 2005.

[4] Balakrishnan, G., Reps, T., Kidd, N., Lal, A., Lim, J., Melski, D., Gruian, R., Yong, S., Chen, C.-H., and Teitelbaum, T., Model checking x86 executables with CodeSurfer/x86 and WPDS++, (tool-demonstration paper). In Proc. Computer-Aided Verification, 2005.

[4] T. Ball and S.K. Rajamani. The SLAM toolkit. In Computer Aided Verif., volume 2102 of Lec. Notes in Comp. Sci., pages 260–264, 2001.

[5] W. Bush, J. Pincus, and D. Sielaff. A static analyzer for finding dynamic programming errors. Software--Practice&Experience, 30:775–802, 2000.

[6] H. Chen, D. Dean, and D. Wagner. Model checking one million lines of C code. In Network and Dist. Syst. Security, 2004.

[7] H. Chen and D. Wagner. MOPS: An infrastructure for examining security properties of software. In Conf. on Comp. and Commun. Sec., pages 235–244, November 2002.

[8] CodeSurfer, GrammaTech, Inc., http://www.grammatech.com/products/codesurfer/.

[9] J.C. Corbett, M.B. Dwyer, J. Hatcliff, S. Laubach, C.S. Pasareanu, Robby, and H. Zheng. Bandera: Extracting finite-state models from Java source code. In Int. Conf. on Softw. Eng., pages 439–448, 2000.

[10] M. Das, S. Lerner, and M. Seigle. ESP: Path-sensitive program verification in polynomial time. In Prog. Lang. Design and Impl., pages 57–68, New York, NY, 2002. ACM Press.

[11] D.R. Engler, B. Chelf, A. Chou, and S. Hallem. Checking system rules using system-specific, programmer-written compiler extensions. In Op. Syst. Design and Impl., pages 1–16, 2000.

[12] K. Havelund and T. Pressburger. Model checking Java programs using Java PathFinder. Softw. Tools for Tech. Transfer, 2(4), 2000.

[13] T.A. Henzinger, R. Jhala, R. Majumdar, and G. Sutre. Lazy abstraction. In Princ. of Prog. Lang., pages 58–70, 2002.

[14] D. Wagner, J. Foster, E. Brewer, and A. Aiken. A first step towards automated detection of buffer overrun vulnerabilities. In Network and Dist. Syst. Security, February 2000.

www.ingramcontent.com/pod-product-compliance
Lightning Source LLC
Chambersburg PA
CBHW082110070326
40689CB00052B/4446